An author can only hope and pra

the way will be challenged to pick up the passion for the subject of their book and pursue it to deeper depths and broader scopes. Such a one has been raised up by God in the person of Susan Dewbrew. While studying my book dealing with God's plan for woman in one of her Christian Leadership University courses, and having already struggled for some time with this issue, God planted in her heart a deep passion to pursue the subject further.

As a result, Susan spent the last fifteen years in research regarding the gender issue. During this time she also laid her heart bare before the Lord seeking a deeper understanding of the Kingdom of God and learning that His Kingdom's solid foundation is love, which leaves no place for fleshly hierarchy of any kind. The results: *Unleashing the Kingdom*, Books 1-3. I have learned so much as I've read these books. Indeed, my student has become my teacher.

Susan hits hard (and I do mean hard) at the centuries of the subjugation of women, but she never once hints that retribution should be the antidote. Rather, she sets the example of gracious forgiveness grounded in love to those who have done the oppressing.

Susan's emphasis on the gospel of the Kingdom is the heart of her teaching in these books. This sometimes elicits the use of some big words and lots of referrals to the Greek and Hebrew. But now and then she inserts some of her humor, making one chuckle in the midst of some heavy point she is making. This gives the reader a peek into her personable, down-to-earth self who is a true lover of Jesus.

These three books that comprise *Unleashing the Kingdom* are each one a must-read for anyone desiring to understand the importance and power of equality for all in the Kingdom of God. In them, Susan also delves into the correct translation of Paul's very misunderstood writings, along with tips on how to hear the voice of God. All three volumes are a treasure trove for anyone with an open heart who is hungry for biblical truth that will deepen their walk with God.

**— JOANNE KRUPP**

AUTHOR OF *WOMAN, GOD'S PLAN NOT MAN'S TRADITION*

I love this series! I love the spirit of it. And I love the revelation truths it has for all of us. Thank you, Susan, for your faithful obedience to both the Word and the Spirit which has produced this incredible gift to the Body of Christ. Thank you, Steve, for putting this gift into such beautiful language.

Twenty years ago, the Lord began to take Susan on a journey revealing His heart for His Bride. Our paths intersected when she enrolled in distance learning classes with our online school, Christian Leadership University. As a graduate student, Susan excelled in her work, and we posted two of her final course papers on our website to be a blessing and resource to others. It is thrilling to see how the Lord used her studies with CLU as a stepping-stone on her journey. We are excited and grateful to God to see the incredible fruit and ministry being born through her life!

With refreshing optimism and not a hint of the feminist Jezebel spirit, Susan invites us to travel with her as she discovers more of God's plan for women, His Church and indeed, the world. In what could potentially be a divisive presentation, Susan's sweet spirit and sincere humility make her message easy to receive, as does her passionate love for Christ and His Church, which comes shining through on every page.

And please note: this is not simply a series about the "women's issues." As important as they are, there is more here than that. The Lord has given Susan a two-fold revelation, which also includes key insights on what it means to be a "king and priest" ruling and reigning with Christ. Her perspective on Kingdom living, what that looks like, and how we should every day bring heaven to earth, is equally powerful. I wholeheartedly agree with this message. The Kingdom of heaven is not a far-off place. As we release Christ and His life and power through our lives in supernatural ways, miracles manifest and *it is done* here on earth as it is in heaven!

Susan is careful to never once let this pure message devolve into male bashing or any spirit of criticism or condemnation. Instead, Susan rightfully declares, "Unity is the key to power, and honor is the key to unity." Indeed, God has been emphasizing 1 Peter 2:17 (NASB) to my heart over and over: we are to "honor all people." *All* people, all mankind, everyone—including women. Susan's teaching on honoring one another's differences (as man and woman) resonates with me because the Lord has been teaching me this as well. To be sure, this message is timely for us all.

Please read these important books with an open mind and most of all with an open heart. Let the Holy Spirit reveal all the Truth He has to share with you on this crucial subject. You will learn things you have never known before. You will come away with a fresh understanding of familiar Scriptures. You will find peace from the tension and questions you've had about women in ministry and leadership. You will be blessed!

**— MARK VIRKLER**

PRESIDENT, CHRISTIAN LEADERSHIP UNIVERSITY
WWW.CLUONLINE.COM

AUTHOR OF OVER 50 BOOKS INCLUDING
*4 KEYS TO HEARING GOD'S VOICE* AND
*OVERFLOW OF THE SPIRIT*

Susan Dewbrew has allowed the Holy Spirit to use her passion for people to write a three-part series of books that points the reader toward the liberating quality of unity. In this work, *Unleashing the*

*Kingdom*, Susan methodically walks you through a well-ordered path of right behavior that can lead you to peace and tranquil living, God's way. She skillfully uses the Holy Scriptures to help the reader understand the tragedy of division and the triumph of God-ordained unity. This is a series of writings that can be used with Bible study groups or individual periods of devotion. You cannot go wrong with this God-inspired work. I offer my most enthusiastic endorsement for *Unleashing the Kingdom*.

— **REVEREND DR. MICHAEL A. EVANS, SR.**
SENIOR PASTOR
BETHLEHEM BAPTIST CHURCH, MANSFIELD, TX

SUSAN DEWBREW
with STEVE PIXLER

# UNLEASHING THE KINGDOM

## TAKING DOMINION THROUGH THE UNITY OF MEN AND WOMEN

CLASH OF KINGDOMS

# UNLEASHING THE KINGDOM

TAKING DOMINION THROUGH THE UNITY OF MEN AND WOMEN

## CLASH OF KINGDOMS


**SUSAN DEWBREW**

WITH STEVE PIXLER



KINGDOM BREWING | MANSFIELD, TX

CREATING & CURATING KINGDOM RESOURCES

**UNLEASHING THE KINGDOM: CLASH OF KINGDOMS (BOOK 2)**



Published in the United States of America by
**Kingdom Brewing** | Mansfield, TX



For distinction, direct scripture quotations are also italicized. All emphasis within scripture quotations are the author's own.

ISBN: 978-1-7372216-1-6

As a matter of honor, this work deliberately capitalizes pronouns referring to the Father, Son, and Holy Spirit. Conversely, the name of satan or any related names or pronouns are intentionally not capitalized.

# CONTENTS

# FOREWORD

## STEVE PIXLER

This book series changed my life. I worked on this project as Susan's ghostwriter—a Holy-Ghost-writer, I've jokingly said!—which is why my name is on the cover. But I was first introduced to Susan's work on women's issues when she and Gregory, her husband and my dear friend, visited our church and shared with me a copy of a small, previous work Susan had published on the topic. Since I am a pastor and writer, people often give me their books to read, and I always flip through the pages dutifully, honoring the time and effort people put into their works. Sometimes a work stands out as special. That's what I sensed immediately with Susan's work. It was unusually special. I read it straight through that afternoon after church.

Throughout the years, I had read countless books on the women's issue, and I was immediately impressed with Susan's clarity, warm style and strong passion that reverberated through every page. But the thing that really captured my attention—that made me sit up with a startled, "Hello!"—was the fact that Susan had really done her homework. As a pastor, amateur theologian and ardent student of Scripture, I pay close attention to how people handle the Word. As I mentioned, I had read volumes of material on the question of women in ministry, and I felt like I had considered the issue from just about every angle. Yet here was Susan, opening up new ways of seeing the Scriptures, and it immediately fascinated me.

Let me give you a little bit of background. I was raised in a super-conservative Pentecostal denomination. As you may know, Pentecostals tend to be an eclectic group, and our corner of the Pentecostal church world was no different. There were all sorts who gathered around the freedom of worship and expression that Pentecostals encouraged, and that freedom to be a bit weird meant that unusual doctrines blew through like March winds.

The question of women in ministry was no different. There were all sorts of opinions and explanations bandied about all my young life. My grandfather and father, both pastors in Fort Worth, TX, disagreed sharply on women in ministry. My grandfather was all for letting women preach, pastor and do anything the men could do. My father, strongly influenced by my mother's childhood pastor, believed that the Scriptures plainly told the women to be silent, though dad was sure that only applied to formal teaching and preaching. Nothing made dad more indignant than being told that he either had to let women preach or make them be totally silent—as in, no singing, amen-ing or teaching Sunday School. Dad would just grunt in disgust at that comeback.

I remember growing up hearing my dad and "Pappy," as I called my grandfather, fuss about "women preachers" for hours on long road trips to regional camp-meetings all over the South. My dad was sure that Paul simply nixed the idea of women in the pulpit, but Pappy was sure that Paul only said women couldn't "usurp authority," as the King James Version put it. "If the pastor lets her preach, James, then she's not usurping authority!" Pappy would protest, his tenor voice rising to the highest register. With my dad all the time shaking his head in stubborn disagreement. "Ain't what it said! Ain't what it said!" And on and on they went, fussing the hours away. My mischievous ten-year-old self loved every minute of it.

When I became a pastor, I embraced my dad's conviction that women are not allowed by Scripture to teach men. They can sing, teach children, be used in the gifts of the Spirit (including prophecy), but they cannot exercise the formal authority of ruling over men from the official seat of judgment, which was the pulpit, as we saw it. I believed it, not just because my dad did, but because I felt like he was right in what he concluded Paul meant. When Paul said that he did not permit women to teach or exercise authority over men, he meant exactly that. And to acquiesce to modern sensibilities just to avoid being considered misogynistic looked like cowardice to me.

After many years of serving as a pastor, my views slowly but surely began to shift. I started taking seriously the varied objections to my settled point of view. I had started shifting on so many legalistic traditions I'd inherited that movement on the women's issue wasn't so much of a leap anymore. But change did prove to be difficult. The first time I invited a women to teach at our church, my father walked out in protest. It was dramatic, people! Though we got everything sorted out between us later, my dad went to his grave believing that I was compromising significant truths that would undermine biblical doctrine. These days, I am comforted by the fact that he is in the presence of the Lord and sees clearly how wrong we all were for so long.

By the time I met Susan and Gregory, I had fully embraced the biblical and spiritual freedom women have to minster alongside men. No doubt, that's what Gregory was "feeling out" when he handed me her book. I later learned that Susan had encountered fierce resistance from many churches and pastors, and they were nervous how I would respond as they visited and considered attending our church. Good thing we met when we did! A few years earlier would have been a different story altogether. Thank God for divine timing.

Regardless, as I have gotten to know Susan, I have been blown away by her honesty and integrity when handling Scripture. Over and over, as we've worked through writing these three books, Susan has insisted on doing more of that careful homework that first drew me into her perspective on the women's issue. I love the fact that she refuses to settle for an inferior explanation that sounds right but isn't. That's what Paul calls "plausible arguments" in Colossians 2:4 (ESV), and Susan flatly refuses to wield them. She will do the work necessary to get what Paul actually said exactly right. And that still makes me sit up and go, "Hello!" with pleasant surprise. I love it.

I think you will too.

One more thing. I am fully committed to the message espoused by this book of unleashing the Kingdom through the unity of men and women. In fact, I am even more committed now after working through each word, each line, each page. I approached this project with curiosity. I have always been eager to learn more about this subject. But through the time we've worked together, I've developed a deeper passion—even a sense of divine mandate!—than I've ever had for this issue. I truly believe that Susan is spot on when she declares that the Kingdom of God cannot fully come in the world as long as the female half of the Church is silenced. The coming of Christ's Kingdom in the right-now, real world is my life-message, so I didn't need much urging to buy into that. The Kingdom message is my sweet spot. But understanding the role of women in advancing the Kingdom and accepting the mandate to advocate for that outcome is a new thing since beginning this project with Susan. As I said, this book series has changed my life. There is a new anointing on my life since reading this book, and I believe the same will happen for you.

Susan and Gregory now attend our church and serve on our Lead Team as Team Leads for our Prayer & Prophetic Team. I've now had the opportunity to work in partnership with them in so many different situations. These people are the real deal, and I fully and highly recommend Susan's work to you. Dive in. Read slow. Back up and read it again. Marinate long in every phrase. Nothing here is wasted. Even portions of the series that seem like we're taking the long way 'round the world are deliberately and prayerfully included to release every layer of revelation that Holy Spirit has graciously commissioned Susan to share with you. Most of all, as you read may "His Kingdom come, His will be done on earth as it is in heaven."

# SERIES INTRODUCTION

## READ ME FIRST!

The human race is divided. And that division begins within the relationship that brings humans into being —the relationship between men and women. Actually, the division starts one level deeper in the breach sin caused between God and people. But in terms of human relationships and the division that plagues the planet, the breakdown between people begins with the breakdown between mom and dad. We learn division at home.

Every human is conceived in a moment of physical oneness that is rarely manifested spiritually beyond the bedroom. Even the best of male and female relations are fractured due to sin, and those fractures work out into human interactions across the social spectrum. As kids grow up, the divide that lies at the heart of fallen families creeps out as suspicion toward neighbors, playmates, kids at school, coworkers and political opponents. The fissures widen into outright hostility, and human relations deteriorate into racism, sexism, ageism, classism, nationalism—and all the other "isms" that force people into warring factions.

This is *the* primary strategy of the enemy. All other demonic strategies flow from this one: "divide and conquer." And because all human division flows from the male-female divide, satan works super-hard to stoke the flames of pride and resentment that foster fear-driven supremacy and subjugation. I am not exaggerating when I say that the division between men and women is the number one item on hell's agenda.

The kingdom of darkness wields global power by exploiting human division, which means that satan must keep men and women snarling at each other's throats in order to keep the pipeline of hate flowing. By "familiating" (to make up a word!) male insecurity and female resentment, the enemy seeks to ensure that every human grows up in a toxic environment of tense competition.

And that idea—that male and female conflict lies at the heart of all human division—is the central idea of this book series. Well, at least it is *half* of the central idea. The other half is that Jesus came to heal human division. He came to bring reconciliation between God and people that would reverse the curse of human division and release shalom into the world—God's peace that heals fractured hearts and makes people whole. Jesus came to release heaven into earth, to *unleash His Kingdom* and transform human society.

> ***Conflict between men and women lies at the heart of all the conflict of the world.***

It is my deepest conviction that Jesus unleashes the Kingdom by healing the rift between men and women. Thus, the Kingdom cannot be fully unleashed as long as men and women remain divided. The Kingdom of God brings healing to the nations, but it begins at home. Better yet, healing begins in the heart, and the transformed heart transforms the home. The transformed home transforms all of human society, for all societal relations are shaped by our *family of origin*.

The curse of sin fell directly on the first male and female on the planet, and when Jesus came to break the curse, He went right to the heart of the matter. The heart of the matter is the *heart*. By reconciling people to God through the cross of Jesus, by regenerating humans through the new birth, by reforming families through saved mom and dads and by reconstituting His Church around these newly healed relations, Jesus releases a new way of being human into all human relations. Young children who grow up in this kind of Kingdom shalom carry healing with them wherever they go. They become world-changers. Jesus is literally changing the world one person at a time. One person at a time becomes one marriage, one family, one church, one city, one nation at a time.

The Kingdom is unleashed when men and women are united. Yet the greatest challenge to male-female unity is male-female equality. As long as men are viewed as superior and women as inferior, true unity is impossible. Men and women can form uneasy alliances, even work together to do loads of good in the world. But the true creational, covenantal unity that reveals the image of God and achieves God-honoring, God-revealing dominion over the earth cannot come as long as one gender dominates the other.

Male supremacy has dominated human society since the Fall of humankind in the Garden of Eden. As Father God mournfully predicted,

> *To the woman He said, "I will greatly multiply your pain in childbirth, in pain you will bring forth children; yet your desire will be for your husband, and he will rule over you." (Genesis 3:16)*

The inevitable consequence of sin, which humans chose, not God, was conflict between men and women. And this is exactly the same curse that Jesus died to break.

I want you to see this, for this is the foundation of everything we will talk about in this series: *conflict between men and women lies at the heart of all the conflict of the world.*

Do you see that? The roots of the curse go back to the relationship between men and women, between parents and children, between God and people. It is silly to say that God saves us from sin and heals our relationship with God, but then leaves us fighting with one another for supremacy. Not at all! The curse came upon male-female relations, and Jesus' death broke that curse *exactly where it started.* Jesus came to heal male-female relations. Is it any wonder that His first miracle was at a wedding?

Now, it will take me a while to prove my point. Three-books-in-a-series-worth of a "while," in fact. (Indeed this entire series just scratches the surface.) The reason it will take some time to prove my point is that we have to sift carefully like archeologists through layers of mindsets and worldviews that have been shaped by millennia of curse-driven concepts. Strata after strata of long-held beliefs that are so deep in our bones that we don't even know that it is a "belief"—we just see it as reality.

The saddest part of all is that the greatest obstacle to gender equality is actually the Church. Not the world—the Church. Or, to put it more exactly, the greatest obstacle to equality is the teachings of the Church that are shaped by cursed culture. We have pietized and religion-ized the awful gender wars pronounced upon man and woman as the inevitable consequence of sin and made them the "Christian" norm.

How did we do this? By misinterpreting and misapplying Scripture. By allowing mindsets imported from the world to shape how we read and teach the Bible. Which means that the only way we can restore creational, covenantal equality to the world is to restore it to the Church, and that can only be done by revisiting and reinterpreting Scripture properly. That will take time. But our commitment to the inspiration and infallibility of Scripture means that we cannot take shortcuts with God's Word. We must take the time to get it right.

And, oddly enough, it is an honest commitment to Scripture that causes part of the confusion. As we shall see, those who teach that women cannot lead in the Church base their conclusions on what appears to be a plain reading of Paul's teaching. And since they believe that they must honor the Word of God—and rightly so!—they advocate the subjugation of women. Many even do so reluctantly. They have no desire to trample women. Or anyone, for that matter.

Many "traditionalists" rightly discern that God's heart beats for the liberation of all suppressed people, especially women, so they celebrate the freedom of women in every way they possibly can in good conscience. But they simply cannot betray what they believe to be true. Honest students of Scripture cannot just dismiss passages that seem to relegate women to a lower status and prohibit them from leadership. There's no doubt that many passages seem to suggest just that.

Pastors and leaders all over the world are working tirelessly to impact their communities with the Kingdom of God, and many have come to understand that the coming of the Kingdom restructures human society. The Kingdom ends slavery. The Kingdom ends economic oppression. The Kingdom ends the exploitation of children. The Kingdom brings transformation to the real world where we live, work and play.

And the pastors and leaders who get this also understand that the Kingdom of God breaks off the yoke of oppression from generations of abused, disempowered and exploited women. Many pastors and leaders have been praying for years for innovative, Spirit-led ways to support and promote women. But some—to put it bluntly—are not sure what to think about it all. Some are torn between what their heart says is true and what their head believes the Bible says. It is a colossal conundrum, to say the least.

It's time to beat a new rhythm on that conundrum.

So what to do? Many leaders feel they must either violate God's heart or violate God's word—an impossible choice. And I feel their pain. I slogged through the same quagmire on my journey. But I have good news! There is no conflict between God's nature and God's Word. We don't have to choose between Scripture and equality for women. It's not an "either-or." Scripture actually *does not* teach the subordination of women. That idea comes from another kingdom, not from the Kingdom of God.

Christian leaders who have the courage to celebrate women—their wives, daughters and female friends—becoming all God created them to be will *love* the revelations emerging from this series because they instinctively know that chauvinism and discrimination violate the *heart* of God. They know that making one group of people "less than" is *not* Christlike. These conflicted, heart-torn pastors and leaders are about to get their prayers answered.

I need to ask you a personal question: *How does this make you feel?* (How you *feel* will control what you receive as you read.)

Think about it for a moment.

Take your emotional pulse.

Does the idea of women in power make you excited or nervous? What do you think when you read statements like "women in authority" or "women in power"? What images come to mind? Do you shudder from the thought of a woman in charge? Did the bottom of your stomach tighten up just a bit?

If so, is it because your dominant perception of women is the Jezebel-type of over-controlling, manipulative female? Or is it because the Bible teaches that women should not have authority over men and therefore should not be in power? Are you fearful of a book that espouses equality for women? Does it sound like "feminism" in the church? Does it sound like heresy or biblical error?

It is important to assess how you feel. If your heart is closed due to fear, it will be almost impossible for Holy Spirit to shift your mind. My prayer is that you will open your heart. Even if it gets uncomfortable for a bit, hang in there.

Trust me, I know how you feel. I have struggled through all the uncertainties and questions that arise with such a daunting subject. I get it. Still, I invite you to take this journey with me. Take a deep breath and relax a bit. I promise it will be worth the trip. And, by the way, I promise that what you learn will be biblically sound. I have no desire to embrace unbiblical ideas either. We all want God's truth. Nothing else.

***We all want God's truth. Nothing else.***

So, in our time together over these three volumes, we will work our way through every significant passage that has been twisted to perpetuate the distortion of gender relations that occurred in the Fall. We will look at:

- 1 Corinthians 14, the "shush your women!" passage
- 1 Corinthians 11, the "headship" passage
- 1 Timothy 2 & 3, the "we don't permit women to teach" and "only men can be elders" passages
- Ephesians 5, the "wives must be subject to their husbands" passage

- Genesis 1 & 2, the "helper" passages

And more.

As we work our way through these passages, I will tell you my story. I will share how Holy Spirit led me through my own personal journey from being a "traditionalist," one who believed that Scripture forbad women from leading or teaching men, to one who came to believe that women are equal to men and can thus teach and lead men without restriction. And I came to believe this *through* Scripture—*because of Scripture!*—not in spite of it.

But throughout each book, we will do so much more than just work through the Scripture passages and tell my story. That will be fun all by itself, but the underlying message of the Kingdom of God will be the glue that binds the pages together. This series is not just about the liberation of women. It is about the liberation of the entire creation through the unleashing of the Kingdom. The gospel of the Kingdom is the overarching theme that will enliven every personal experience and every Scripture interpretation.

Here's how we will continue the series as we carry on with Book 2.

- In Book 1, we set the table. I shared my personal experience with my journey from the traditional view of "The Woman's Place" to where I currently stand. And I started working through some of the biblical passages that need to be addressed—specifically 1 Corinthians 14, the "shush your women!" passage.
- Then, we wrapped up Book 1 with a quick segue into the gospel of the Kingdom. We are now ready for Book 2, where the "Clash of Kingdoms" will be front and center. We will take the time in Book 2 to make sure that the Kingdom message penetrates down to the cellular level in our hearts.

- Finally, in Book 3, we will dig deep into the "proof texts" that are used and misused to ban women from leadership in the Church and in the world. We will talk about "Lies That Bind" and false filters that distort how we see Scripture.

As you might expect, all three books are essential to the overall message of *Unleashing the Kingdom*. Each book can be read as a free-standing volume. But in order to get the big picture, it's best to read all three in full and in order. We developed the volumes as a trilogy to make them more "digestible," rather than publishing one, intimidating monster manuscript. Hope that helps!

One final thing before we start. This series is not only about women's liberation—this is a series about human liberation. And human liberation is the liberation of both men and women released as the image of God working together in unity. Ironically, men are subjugated by the subjugation of women. Just as enslaving others is its own form of slavery—sometimes the slave is more free than the master—so male superiority is its own form of inferiority. Men who are truly free have no need to dominate anyone. Male domination, then, is an open admission of male insecurity. Raw power is always rooted in fear.

Moreover, God made men and women to be fully alive through union. In other words, men cannot be fully *men* without women. That doesn't mean that every man must be married, but it does mean that men must be properly aligned to women as a gender in order to be fully who God created men to be.

We are all social creatures by design. We cannot be fully who we were meant to be without healthy alignment with others. The hammer is useless without the nail. The glove has no purpose without the hand. The instrument has no melody without the musician. On and on—examples of essential union abound. The point is clear: God made men and women for union, and when one oppresses the other, both suffer.

So this series is not just about liberating women. It is about liberating *everyone*. It is about helping humans find the purpose for which God made us all. It is about unleashing the Kingdom in the world so that salvation may come to the nations. And the Kingdom cannot be unleashed as long as half of its citizens are subjugated.

But here I am getting ahead of myself and telling you all I need to tell you over three volumes. So let me stop here and invite you to take a journey with me. A journey that will empower both men and women, break the demonic division that grips our world and unleash the Kingdom of God in every nation under heaven. Sound ambitious? It is. But it is an ambition worth pursuing.

Ready?

Let's get started.

# UNLEASHING THE KINGDOM
# (BOOK 2)

## CLASH OF KINGDOMS

# CHAPTER 1

# BUCKLE YOUR SEAT BELT

The world is changing. There is a move of God being unleashed throughout the earth, and it is shifting the balance of power that has dominated human society for millennia. The Kingdom of God is being unleashed.

This sets up an epic clash of kingdoms, a cosmic war between the Kingdom of God and the kingdom of darkness. The kingdom of darkness held sway over the human race until Jesus came and brought heaven to earth. When the incarnate Christ descended into human history, He unleashed the rule of heaven on earth. After Jesus died, rose again and ascended into heaven, He was enthroned as King over all creation. Then, He poured out His kingly Spirit at Pentecost and released the Spirit of heaven into the world through Spirit-filled people. The Kingdom of God took root in regenerated humans and through them started flowing out into the real world where humans live, work and play. The Kingdom within became the Kingdom without as changed people changed the world.

## *Divide and Conquer*

Prior to the victory of Christ, the kingdom of darkness held sway over the human race through division. By dividing humans into sub-groups and setting them against one another—the age-old "divide and conquer" strategy—satan successfully dominated world history before Jesus came. So, when Jesus came, He struck at the heart of demonic power by striking at the hostility that divided us. By making peace at the cross, Jesus reconciled humans to God, and through that reconciliation, reconciled us to one another. By re-connecting human identity to the image of God rather than to the factions that divide us, Jesus laid the foundation for a new way of being human and a new way of forming human society. The old divisions are obliterated in Christ, and the new unity-in-diversity that celebrates individuality-in-community now defines what it means to be truly human together.

Hate is inhuman. Bigotry is inhuman. Racism is inhuman. Sexism is inhuman. Ageism is inhuman. Any other "ism's" I've missed? Every "ism" that divides humans is a "schism," and all schisms have been cancelled by the cross. The Kingdom of God declared war on the kingdom of darkness, and one soul at a time is being liberated from the lies that broke us apart and ghettoized human existence.

***The move of God that's happening is a unity through identity movement that totally reorganizes the structures of human society.***

The move of God that's happening is a *unity through identity* movement that totally reorganizes the structures of human society. By bringing people into the true *identity* for which they were created, the identity hidden for them in Christ before the foundation of the world, Holy Spirit is forging a new human *unity* rooted in the reconciliation purchased for us by Christ at the cross. Our reconciliation with God produces reconciliation with one another.

As Paul put it,

> *For you are all sons of God through faith in Christ Jesus. For all of you who were baptized into Christ have clothed yourselves with Christ. There is neither Jew nor Greek, there is neither slave nor free man, there is neither male nor female; for you are all one in Christ Jesus. And if you belong to Christ, then you are Abraham's descendants, heirs according to promise. (Galatians 3:26–29)*

When we become sons of God through faith, we are submerged into Christ and emerge as the new self we were created to be in Him. We are "clothed" with Christ. In our new identity, we arise to live out a new human oneness formed in Christ. Now, in Christ, all human divisions are broken down. Jew and Greek, slave and free, male and female all become one in Christ.

This unity is a "unity-in-diversity" that celebrates individuality without exclusion. The unity formed in Christ is *not* a bland unity-through-uniformity that suppresses uniqueness and individuality. Not at all. It is only as each regenerated individual discovers their identity in Christ that the manifold glory of God is manifest. It takes a "a great multitude which no one could count" to fully manifest the glory of God. (Revelation 7:9) Each person is like a vibrant thread woven together to form the cosmic tapestry that reveals the universal image of God. It takes each thread in its individual glory to display the overall picture.

The tear in the cosmic tapestry started with Adam and Eve. It started with a division between man and woman and then worked its way out from there. By rooting human division in the original human relationship of male and female—which is the relationship from which *all* relationships spring—satan fiendishly wove division into the warp and woof, the threads that form the fabric, of human society. All human division flows from the division between mom and dad. And this is why I insist that the Kingdom of God must get to the root of division, to the rips and tears that fray male and female relations, so that unity can flow out into every other area of division.

The unleashed Kingdom that transforms the world starts in the transformed relations between men and women. We cannot expect the Kingdom to change the world at the highest levels of society if we are not willing to let it change us at home. Moreover, we cannot expect the unleashed Kingdom to change the world if it does not first change the Church. Male and female relationships will be permanently transformed only when the Church realizes its essential role in mediating reconciliation between men and women. The Church must reject the centuries-old traditions that have institutionalized and ecclesiastical-ized division through the oppression of women.

Here's the point: the Kingdom of God is unleashed in the world when women are unleashed. The clash between kingdoms is sure to favor the kingdom of darkness as long as half the warriors in Christ's Kingdom—the female ones!—are subdued and silenced. Women *must* be unleashed. We cannot celebrate the liberation of slaves, of all races, of all ethnic groups and nationalities while still justifying the suppression of women.

As we demonstrate carefully throughout this book series, there is no biblical justification for preserving the ancient ban on women leading, teaching and guiding the Church. And my objective in Book 2 of this series, the one you're now reading, is to show how the gospel of the Kingdom is absolutely essential in the quest for equality. The Kingdom is actually a big deal.

## *My Story*

In Book 1, I shared much of my story. As you may remember, I started my journey from a traditional vantage point, convinced that women could not lead with biblical sanction. The Bible clearly said no, I thought, so that's that. But that wasn't that after all. I shared how Holy Spirit led me through many years of exploration, what seemed like lifetimes of mixed signals, working hard to understand the conflict between what I felt from the heart of God and what I read in Scripture. I was torn between God's heart and God's Word, and that is an impossible place to dwell—at least for me and others who truly believe that the Bible is God's divinely inspired Word.

Thankfully, over the course of several years, I kept hearing clear words from the Lord that guided my quest for understanding. He first asked me, "Why did I send Mary?" which totally rocked my world. Why *did* He send Mary? If women are forbidden to speak, why did He send a woman to preach the first Easter message? That took me to a dark place for a while as I tried futilely to explain the "prohibition scriptures." I can't retell the story here—I tell it in vivid detail in Book 1—but it was wild ride.

A few years into the journey, and I had the "she has Chaldee!" dream that made so little sense that I was more confused after than before. But again, with time, Holy Spirit led me into the mind-blowing revelation that "Chaldee" was a spirit of misogyny indigenous to Babylon, that ancient nemesis of Christ's Kingdom, that had worked its way through the Hebrew Talmud into Pharisaic Judaism and thus into the early Church.[1] That took me through years of research on Christian feminism, "Women's Lib" and frustrating achievement gaps between men and women. I worked like crazy trying to understand it all.

Then a powerful key dropped in my lap when I read a work by Professor Joanne Krupp that introduced (to me) the idea that Paul *did not* teach women in Corinth to be silent. Paul was actually quoting a false teacher whose words were included in a letter that the Corinthians had sent to Paul.

Ever heard that? No? Then, take the time to read Book 1 in this series and work through it with me. It's a powerful perspective that restores Paul's original desire to promote equality for women and prevents us from getting vertigo when we read Paul's apparently (but not actually) schizophrenic opinions on women.

***The move of God that's happening is a unity through identity movement that totally reorganizes the structures of human society.***

After reading Professor Krupp, my heart was broken. In fact, I was enraged, furious that generations of women over nearly two thousand years of Church history had been wrongfully oppressed through a false reading of Paul's teaching. I was even somewhat offended at God for a moment. How could He let that happen? But Holy Spirit arrested my outrage with a surprising statement:

---

[1] Misogyny is the "dislike of, contempt for, or ingrained prejudice against women." (New Oxford American Dictionary) Dictionary.com defines misogyny as "hatred, dislike, or mistrust of women, manifested in various forms such as physical intimidation and abuse, sexual harassment and rape, social shunning and ostracism, etc.; ingrained and institutionalized prejudice against women; sexism."

"The hearts of men are now ready."

Say what?! What does that have to do with why God allowed millennia of oppression supported with spurious biblical authority? But I just love how God answers overwrought questions with seemingly irrelevant statements. Once my heart settled down into the word, "The hearts of men are now ready," the anger evaporated. I caught a glimpse of the long-view of the Kingdom, of God's providential outworking of His will. I saw how God is preparing my generation for a renaissance of equality for men and women that would unleash the Kingdom like never before.

And right when I was leveling out in high gear, ready to reinterpret every passage that had even been misused to oppress women, Holy Spirit yanked the wheel hard right, and I took an unannounced and unexpected detour into a five-year Kingdom hiatus. Father God wanted to show me something much more important than correct interpretation of the scriptures related to women leading: He wanted to show me how the Kingdom transforms *all* relationships and becomes the foundation for right relations in all of life.

So, that's what we're doing in Book 2. We are going off-road. We are going on a grand adventure, four-wheeling our way through the wilderness of Kingdom revelation. And you will find just as I did, that this unexpected journey is not a detour after all—the Kingdom *is* the destination!

It's going to be amazing. Buckle up.

# CHAPTER 2

# THE KINGDOM HAS COME

Jesus came to liberate women. Actually, He came to liberate everyone, and women are part of everyone, but I mean specifically that Jesus came to break the curse that subjugated women under male supremacy.

Jesus purposefully brought liberation to the women around Him, and so did Paul. They challenged the status quo and overturned generations of misogyny. The freedom that women now enjoy started two-thousand years ago when Jesus gathered women around Him and preached to them the gospel of the Kingdom.

Yet Christianity has not fully lived up to the hopeful promise of the gospel. As we recounted in painful detail throughout Book 1, there is still an underlying belief within the Church that women are subordinate to men, especially married women to their husbands. And this persistent misunderstanding flows out of an even deeper misunderstanding about the Kingdom.

Get this: to understand the liberation of women we must understand the Kingdom and how the Kingdom could *never* sustain a system of male supremacy.

That may sound strange at first. It certainly did to me. As I told you above, I was rocked by what I saw in Professor Krupp's book on 1 Corinthians 14. I couldn't believe that women had suffered so much due to an egregious misinterpretation of Scripture. Then, in the middle of my outrage, I heard God declare, "The hearts of men are now ready." That broke the anger I felt and set me up for the next phase of my journey, which was a complete recalibration of my perspective on the Kingdom.

It seemed at first like a detour. I was just discovering truths about equality for women that I had felt in my gut for years but could not defend in light of the prohibition passages. And now, just as I was getting to the heart of the matter, this "Kingdom message" starting cutting in like interference on an old AM radio.

Holy Spirit told me that I had to grasp the truth about the Kingdom before I could fully understand the women's issue. He told me that skipping a revelation of the Kingdom would be like skipping over addition and subtraction because you want to learn algebra. You can't understand one without the other.

So the Kingdom it is.

## *The Gospel of the Kingdom*

If you grew up in church, you probably believe the primary reason Jesus came to earth was to pay the penalty for our sins. And He did indeed do that. However, as shocking as this may sound, Jesus' main message was not the "gospel of salvation." Jesus did not come to earth just to save a few lost souls from hell so that He could take them all to heaven someday. Jesus did deal with the sin problem, but that was a means to an end. Jesus dealt with sin so that humans could be reconciled to God and restored to their rightful place as co-rulers with God over all creation. Jesus came to realign human dominion with the Kingdom of Heaven. Jesus came to put humans back on the throne with God. (Revelation 3:21)

Salvation was the means to restoring the Kingdom.

Jesus came to restore our original identity as image-bearing kings. We were created to be one with God and one with each other. Jesus' purpose as the second Adam was to reinstate the original plan in the Garden: to have intimacy with God and each other and, from that place of unity, to exercise dominion over the earth. The Kingdom is the *King's dominion*, and that dominion was shared with humans when they were placed in the garden as the living, breathing image of God. The King made us kings with Him.

As Psalm 115 says,

> *But our God is in the heavens; He does whatever He pleases. (Psalm 115:3)*

And then,

> *The heavens are the heavens of the Lord, but the earth He has given to the sons of men. (Psalm 115:16)*

Verse three is a powerful statement of God's absolute sovereignty. But verse sixteen declares what the Sovereign Lord decided to do with His sovereignty: He shared it with us. Specifically, God delegated Kingdom authority over the earth to humans. The King made us kings.

Psalm 8 declares,

> *O Lord, our Lord, How majestic is Your name in all the earth, who have displayed Your splendor above the heavens! From the mouth of infants and nursing babes You have established strength because of Your adversaries, to make the enemy and the revengeful cease.*
>
> *When I consider Your heavens, the work of Your fingers, the moon and the stars, which You have ordained; what is man that You take thought of him, and the son of man that You care for him? Yet You have made him a little lower than God, and You crown him with glory and majesty!*
>
> *You make him to rule over the works of Your hands; You have put all things under his feet, all sheep and oxen, and also the beasts of the field, the birds of the heavens and the fish of the sea, whatever passes through the paths*

*of the seas. O Lord, our Lord, how majestic is Your name in all the earth! (Psalm 8:1–9)*

When humans sinned in the garden their union with God was disrupted, but God never revoked the dominion mandate given to Adam and Eve. Through sin humans granted the enemy permission to work in the world, but human dominion was never lost. Moreover, God never recognized the usurper's right to rule over the earth, and Jesus came to destroy the works of the devil and restore man's righteous rule over creation. Jesus came to recover our lost identity as sons and daughters of God, as kings over the earth.

This is why Jesus came preaching the "gospel of the Kingdom."[1] Though Jesus forgave our sins, His primary focus was not our sin. His primary focus was our intrinsic value to the Father (think of the one lost lamb) and our restored relationship with Him. Jesus came to restore us to honor and glory.

> ***When humans sinned in the garden their union with God was disrupted, but God never revoked the dominion mandate given to Adam and Eve.***

Sin was just an enemy to be defeated, a cancer to be removed. Jesus knew so well that a restored relationship with God not only resolved the sin problem, but it also released the love of God that graciously transforms the world through us.

The word "gospel" means "good news." The "gospel of the Kingdom" is indeed good news. The "good news of the Kingdom" is that the King of all creation came to earth as a

[1] Matthew 4:23, 9:35, 24:14, Mark 1:15, Luke 16:16.

human to recover divine-human kingship over the earth. The King of kings defeated the enemy and stripped him of all stolen human authority. All the evil powers, often called "the Principalities and Powers," were defeated and dethroned at the cross. As Paul said,

> *When [God] had disarmed the rulers and authorities, He made a public display of them, having triumphed over them through [Jesus]. (Colossians 2:15)*

Salvation is much bigger than just being forgiven of sin and granted access to heaven when you die. Salvation is the recovery and restoration of all that was lost due to sin. Salvation is new creation, this old creation made new. By healing the breach that satan's lies caused between God and people, Jesus opened the way for humans to be seated with Christ in heavenly places upon Kingdom thrones. (Ephesians 2:6)

Most Christians have been taught that Jesus came to save us from our sins so we can go to heaven when we die and that's when the Kingdom will come. But that simply is not true. Jesus made it clear that He came to release the Kingdom of God in the earth *right now*. By saving us from our sins, Jesus healed the human heart and made the heart the portal of the Kingdom through which transformation would come into the world.

## *The Kingdom Is Here and Now*

Think about this now:

(1) Jesus broke the power of sin at the Cross and reconciled us to God so that we could be restored to our partnership with God as kings over the earth.

(2) Jesus ascended into heaven as a glorified human so that humans could be elevated to reign with Him from the throne of God over *all creation.*

(3) Jesus poured out the Holy Spirit so that the Kingly Spirit of Almighty God could take root in the human heart and release transformation into the world through love.

And all that is happening *now!* The prayer Jesus taught us petitions the Father now, "Your Kingdom come. Your will be done in earth as it is in heaven." The prayer is not that the Kingdom will come someday when we all get to heaven. No! The prayer is that the Kingdom will come here and now on earth as it already is in heaven.

What is coming has already come. As Hebrews says, the Holy Spirit, whom we receive now, is "the power of the age to come" (Hebrews 6:5). Jesus brought the future into the present when He rose from the dead in the middle of human history. By filling us with His Spirit, He invested the Kingdom in us now. As Paul said,

> *For the kingdom of God is not eating and drinking, but righteousness and peace and joy in the Holy Spirit. (Romans 14:17)*

Jesus also said that the Kingdom is within us:

> *Now having been questioned by the Pharisees as to when the kingdom of God was coming, He answered them and said, "The kingdom of God is not coming with signs to be observed; nor will they say, 'Look, here it is!' or, 'There it is!' For behold, the kingdom of God is in your midst." (Luke 17:20–21)*

(The margin note in the NASB on that last phrase is "the kingdom of God is within you.")

The Kingdom of God is the Spirit of the future age coming into the present and restoring the past. The Church must reject eschatologies that postpone the Kingdom to any time in the future. The future is now.

Why does this matter? Because Kingdom reality—what was lost through sin and what is coming through salvation—is already present *right now*. This means that we must live life now according the original pattern by which God made the world. The Kingdom redeems *history* and guarantees *destiny*.

The revelation of the Kingdom on earth right here, right now has a profound impact on relations between men and women. Since the Kingdom has broken in upon the world, male-female relations must be redefined in terms of how God made the world at the beginning and what He intends the world to become. Male and female relations must not be determined by fallen human culture. The King and His Kingdom establishes the norms for human behavior.

That's why the Kingdom matters.

Jesus' message was simple: "Repent! The Kingdom of Heaven is at hand" (Matthew 4:17). (By the way, "the Kingdom of God and the Kingdom of Heaven are interchangeable terms, not two distinct realities as some teach.) The Kingdom message was exactly what John the Baptist preached. It was the message that the disciples were commissioned to preach. Jesus sent His disciples out on missions with these instructions:

> *And as you go, preach, saying, "The kingdom of heaven is at hand." Heal the sick, raise the dead, cleanse the lepers, cast out demons. Freely you received, freely give. (Matthew 10:7-8)*

Jesus and His disciples healed the sick as a sign of the present Kingdom. Since there is no sickness in heaven, they displayed the reality of heaven on earth by healing sickness. When someone was healed or delivered by the Spirit of God,

Jesus would proclaim: "The Kingdom has come upon you" (Matthew 12:28; see also Luke 11:20).

When Jesus healed the sick, cast out demons, cleansed the lepers and raised the dead, He was demonstrating the present reality of the Kingdom. The Kingdom of God transforms the world wherever it goes. That is indeed good news!

Many religious leaders in Jesus' day thought that sickness was caused directly by sin. If you were sick, then you had sinned. When Jesus healed the sick, those leaders accused Jesus of being in cahoots with the devil:

> *But when the Pharisees heard this, they said, "This man casts out demons only by Beelzebul the ruler of the demons."*
>
> *And knowing their thoughts Jesus said to them, "Any kingdom divided against itself is laid waste; and any city or house divided against itself will not stand. If Satan casts out Satan, he is divided against himself; how then will his kingdom stand?*
>
> *If I by Beelzebul cast out demons, by whom do your sons cast them out? For this reason they will be your judges. But if I cast out demons by the Spirit of God, then the kingdom of God has come upon you. (Matthew 12:24–28)*

Jesus responded to the Pharisees' slander by pointing out a powerful revelation: expelling demons is a sign that the Kingdom has come. Healing the sick, casting out demons, raising the dead, cleansing the lepers—on and on—means that *the Kingdom of God is here right now.* The Kingdom of God is present and changing the world.

## *Seeing the Kingdom*

One of the greatest signs in our day that the Kingdom is present right here, right now, is the ongoing transformation of male and female relations. The modern suffragist and feminist movement has appeared to many Christians as the devil's work, but they are mistaken. While it is true that satan has attempted to highjack and co-opt the women's movement, corrupting it with sexual perversion, gender confusion and abortion rights, yet God, as always, has His way in the whirlwind. The Kingdom of God is working out God's vision of reality by any means necessary, and sometimes the Kingdom comes outside the rigid structures of institutional Christianity. It is rather sad, when you think about it, that the most forceful opponents of liberation for women have been church leaders.

> ***The most forceful opponents of liberation for women have been church leaders.***

Yet, in spite of fierce resistance from calcified religion, the Kingdom of God has been shifting the balance of power and reorienting society. The Kingdom has been at work in the world like yeast in the dough. (Matthew 13:33) There is much to be sorted out, a lot of confusion to be strained out of the mix, but never doubt it for a moment: the Kingdom of God will triumph, and Abba's daughters will be free.

The Kingdom of God comes in the earth as it is in heaven. Jesus healed the sick because there is no sickness in heaven. He cast out demons because demons have no power to enslave in heaven. Jesus fed the hungry because there is no hunger in heaven. Jesus forgave sins because there is no sin in heaven. And just so, Jesus welcomed women because there is no contempt for women in heaven. There is no male supremacy in heaven. Therefore, as the Kingdom comes on earth, equality for women is inevitable. As the Kingdom comes, as His will is done in earth as it is in heaven, the oppression of women must cease.

If we believe that the Kingdom is some future, remote reality, then we will continue to live on earth enslaved under the wrong kingdom.[2] If we believe that our only experience of heaven right now is "Jesus in our heart" and that our greatest hope is to "go to heaven when we die"; if we believe that the Kingdom has no real impact outside our personal piety right now; then we will resign ourselves to the false reality of a world in the grip of sin and death and hope for a better future some day when Jesus comes again. And that's exactly what the Church has done for generations with regard to the women's issue.

It is amazing how many Christians were born again as citizens of Heaven and yet continue to live like slaves of hell. Jesus brought to us an entirely new way of being human, but too many of us are still living in the old self, in the old world. It's time to be "born again, again," to actually enter the Kingdom of God in reality and not just theory. And when we do, our view of male superiority and female subjugation will radically change, for there is no hierarchy of worth in the Kingdom of God.

"Seeing the Kingdom," as Jesus put it in John 3, is all about receiving a revelation of how the Kingdom transforms the world. And "seeing the Kingdom" requires a "Spirit of wisdom and revelation" (Ephesians 1:17) that opens the eyes of our heart to see what God is doing in the world and how

---

[2] "Wrong kingdom" has become shorthand for me to identify ideas that come from the kingdom of darkness. You'll see me use it often throughout this series.

He is doing it. We need Holy Spirit to open our eyes to what God is doing even when it seems so counterintuitive and outside the box.

In fact, if you know how God works at all, you know that He usually works outside our sense of propriety and decorum. He loves to shock our sensibilities and offend our religious systems. Jesus still wades through our crowded temples overthrowing tables and casting out religious merchandisers.

Jesus is an iconoclast. There is no greater fury in the universe than God's fury against idols. He smashes vain pretensions and exposes smug hypocrisy. He sneers at religious ritual and flouts orthodox conventions. He is a Man on a mission, determined to save His creation from the curse. Jesus will work in the world through whatever means necessary. He loves His Church—and He loves you!—but He has no patience with religion.

If we want to see equality, we must *see the Kingdom*. We must see how the unleashed Kingdom unleashes an entirely new way of being human, an entirely new way of interacting as male and female. Let's take a closer look.

# CHAPTER 3

# LOVE, NOT POWER

What is a kingdom?

A kingdom is a king's domain. It is the sphere in which a monarch has power and authority. It is his or her jurisdiction, the territory where he or she has the right to rule. The boundaries of the monarch's kingdom define the limits of rule. The Queen of England rules over her domain: the United Kingdom and the English Commonwealth. However, her rule is limited. She has no authority beyond her borders. She may visit the United States and receive high honor while here. But she has no say in what happens. The US is not her domain.

The same is true of our President. He or she governs within the limits established by our Constitution, and he or she has no authority beyond our borders. He or she may visit the UK and celebrate our "Special Relationship" with Great Britain, but he or she has no authority over the English while there. His or her "domain" is defined by our national boundaries.

## *The Power of Love*

God is King of all creation. His "domain" is everything. There is no molecule of the universe that does not submit to His Word. Look at Psalm 115:3 again:

> *But our God is in the heavens; He does whatever He pleases. (Psalm 115:3)*

The Psalmist has a high view of God's sovereignty: "He does whatever he pleases." That's pretty broad. Yet, as we saw above, Psalm 115:16 goes on to show that the sovereign King willingly limited His own sovereignty when He delegated authority to humans:

> *The heavens are the heavens of the Lord, but the earth He has given to the sons of men. (Psalm 115:16)*

Now, this is *profoundly* important to understanding how the Kingdom works and how the Kingdom redefines male and female relations. Get this:

God has all power yet freely chooses to limit his power through love.

Love is God's boundary, His only limit. His "domain" is defined by love. God, the only one who actually has enough power to make people do whatever He wants, is the only one who has never attempted it. Why is that? Because God is love, and His Kingdom operates through love, not power.

> ***God, the only one who actually has enough power to make people do whatever He wants, is the only one who has never attempted it.***

The kingdoms of the world are formed around *power structures*. As Jesus said,

> *"The kings of the Gentiles lord it over them; and those who have authority over them are called 'Benefactors.' But it is not this way with you, but the one who is the greatest among you must become like the youngest, and the leader like the servant." (Luke 22:25–26)*

This is one of the clearest contrasts in Scripture between how the kingdoms of the world operate versus the Kingdom of God. And the contrast is simply the difference between *power* and *love*. "God is love" (1 John 4:8). Therefore, God's *power* is an expression of His *love.* Which means that "the mighty power of God" is not the same sort of "power" that the world wields. In fact, the power of God and the power of the world are so different that we need new language to define the difference. Maybe we should call God's power "love-power" to distinguish God's power from the world's power.

God's love-power is the most powerful force in the universe, yet it never uses *force*. The power of God's love-power created the universe. The sun, moon and stars; the planets, the seas, the mountains; everything formed flowed out of the boundless love-power of God. Creation came into being from the abundant overflow of the Father's love. God *gave* and all things *became*. That's true love-power. That's *influence-ment*, not *enforcement*.

The power of the world operates out of *lust,* not *love.* The world's power is a self-centered power that takes, not gives. It is a parasitic power that drains life and energy from people. The world's power uses people for its own advancement. The power of God flows from His love to empower people, not exploit them. The power of God gives, not takes. It is love, not lust. The Kingdom of God, then, operates out of *love-power, not lust-power.*

What does that mean in practical terms? It means that God influences people to change by loving them, not by controlling them. This is why the first humans in the garden were given clear instructions and then leeway to make their own choice. God's highest ideal is love, and love requires freedom. Freedom requires choice.

This is why the world is the sort of world it is, a world where God does not prevent every bad thing from happening. If God prevented all evil, the world would not be free and love would not be possible. God wants us to know His love more than anything. Therefore, He does not dominate us—He liberates us through love.

The Kingdom of God works through love. This is why Jesus decried the violence that motivated the Zealots of His day. They sought to advance God's Kingdom, the Kingdom foretold by the prophets, through political, economic and military force. They thought they could manifest the Kingdom through violence.

But Jesus exposed the lie at the heart of violent revolution when He submitted willingly to the most extreme form of violence at the cross and broke its power through love. Death is an enemy, not a strategy. Violence is a hoax. It is a lie told by satan as he deludes humans into an evil alliance through revenge, revolution and murder.

Suppression, oppression, every form of human subjugation, is rooted in a "power-myth," the idea that we get ahead by putting others down. This is the lie of supremacy: white supremacy, male supremacy, religious supremacy or any other form of supremacy. It's rooted in fear, driven by pride and invariably ends in murder.

Do you see how understanding the love-powered Kingdom transforms the way we see male and female relations?

The Kingdom of God advances in the world by influencing our heart, not by controlling our actions. Even though He does not need it, God wants our agreement. He will never force Himself on us.

God works out His will by loving us. When He loves us, we love Him in return. (1 John 4:19) That's the transformative power of His love—freedom, not force. When He loves us, His love draws our heart into agreement with

His. His heart and our heart begin to beat as one. We do His will now because we freely choose to do so out of love.

## *Love Gives A Choice*

Of course, the harsh reality of freedom means that many people refuse God's love and rebel against His will. And that means—get ready for a shocker!—God does not always get what He wants. For example, God desires all people to be saved (1 Timothy 2:4), but all people are *not* being saved. As Peter said, God is "not wishing for any to perish but for all to come to repentance" (2 Peter 3:9). But "all" are not coming to repentance, a fact that deeply grieves our Father's heart.

Yet Father God refuses to force anyone. He loves and His love transforms. But He will not force our compliance.

Think about it now: God is the Supreme Being of the universe. If anyone has the right to "supremacy," it is Him. Yet He refuses to exercise that right. In fact, He deliberately set aside His divine prerogatives just to show us what love looks like. Paul described it like this:

> *Have this attitude in yourselves which was also in Christ Jesus, who, although He existed in the form of God, did not regard equality with God a thing to be grasped, but emptied Himself, taking the form of a bond-servant, and being made in the likeness of men. Being found in appearance as a man, He humbled Himself by becoming obedient to the point of death, even death on a cross.*
>
> *For this reason also, God highly exalted Him, and bestowed on Him the name which is above every name, so that at the name of Jesus every knee will bow, of those who are in heaven and on earth and under the earth, and that every tongue will confess that Jesus Christ is Lord, to the glory of God the Father. (Philippians 2:5–11)*

Jesus deliberately laid aside His "supremacy" to show us what love is like. God doesn't automatically get what He wants just because He is God. He could have made us robots who simply obey Him, but He did not. He desires a genuine, passionate love relationship with us. He wants our heart.

God is love. And as Perfect Love, He exists eternally in community as the Triune God. God the Father, Son and Holy Spirit model perfectly through Their exquisite unity-in-diversity what human relations should look like. The "perichoresis" of divine love—the "circle dance" of interpenetration, which is what that $5 word means—requires zero supremacy and subjugation. The divine love flows in perfect freedom. No coercion, just willing surrender to one another.

***Love by definition always presents a choice. If you are not free to choose, then it's not love.***

And that's what male and female relations are meant to be. A perichoresis of mutual submission.

God is not a chauvinist. He desires our heart. He longs intensely to love us, but He refuses to coerce us. He woos us, draws us, influences us, but He does not force us. "The kindness of God leads you to repentance" (Romans 2:4).

The sovereign will of God is worked out in us through love. The will of $God is both His desire and His intent, and He infuses His will into our heart through the indwelling of His Spirit within us. His will is an expression of His love. So as He loves us, His will impregnates our will, and we give birth to divine desire. And it all happens so beautifully through willing surrender.

Love by definition always presents a choice. If you are not free to choose, then it's not love. True love does not seek its own benefit over that of another. Rather, love always gives of itself. Love does not manipulate people to gratify its own desires and seek its own promotion. Instead, love reaches out to lift others up. The incredible brilliance of this divine strategy is the more people operate in love, the higher we all go. A rising tide lifts all boats.

*Love cannot be compelled or coerced. If "love" is forced, it is not love—it is rape.*

## *A Battle For the Heart*

God is after your heart. In the battle that rages between good and evil, the prize is your heart. The battlefield is in your mind, but the territory contested is your heart.

Why is there such a battle for the human heart? Simply because God gave humans dominion over the earth, and the human heart determines human history. Everything—thoughts, words and behavior—flows from the human heart. As Jesus said,

> *For out of the heart come evil thoughts, murders, adulteries, fornications, thefts, false witness, slanders. (Matthew 15:19)*

God wants our heart because He loves people and He loves His good creation:

> *"God so loved the world that He gave His only begotten Son..." (John 3:16)*

God wants our heart for relationship. That is what He created us for from the beginning.

Satan, however, wants our heart so he can dominate us. He seeks control over the human race so he can control the world. His lustful, insatiable desire for humans is to make them pawns on his chessboard. Satan seeks power. And that's why the kingdoms of the world operate solely through the brutal imposition of power. They are "of [their] father, the devil," as Jesus put it. (John 8:44)

In order for satan to get his way on the earth, he must delude humans into compliance. He tells big, fat lies that appeal to shortsighted human self-interest and persuades people to align with his will. Once people believe the lie, satan's power over them deepens into spiritual control. Satan's domination of humans can become so complete that people need deliverance in order to break free of satan's lies.

Satan can do nothing on his own. He relies totally on our tacit and explicit cooperation. Humans live out of their hearts. That's where emotions are felt, decisions are made and mindsets are shaped. In order for satan to control human destiny, he must gain control of the human heart.

The same is true for God, though it's never a matter of control for Him. For God, it's a matter of liberating the human will to become all it was created to be as the image of God. When God liberates the human will, it is set free to become what it originally was when humans were formed in the image and likeness of God. When God showers His love upon us and liberates our will, we do the will of God willingly because that's what the human will was first formed to do. Salvation restores us to our original human nature, which manifests freely the nature of God.

This is why God does not need to coerce us. All He must do is love us, and when He loves us, He liberates us to be what we were created to be. That's not force—that's freedom!

It is astonishing to consider how the King of all creation shows such honor toward us. Of course, He wants His will done on earth, but He will not force it on us. He is powerful enough to make us obey if He wanted, and He is certainly smart enough to manipulate us. However, that is not how love behaves.

My husband, Gregory, has a simple but profound life message: "It's a get-to, not a have-to." That changes everything! Are you choosing to obey God out of a sense of duty? Or do you genuinely "get-to"? Does the motive even matter as long as you are doing what God wants? You bet it does! Everything in the Kingdom circles back to the heart. So even when you do the right thing, if you do it for the wrong reason you will miss the mark. This is a key to the Kingdom.

### *Love One Another*

Let me wrap up this chapter with one more level to this "love, not power" idea—the "you-and-me" level.

God wants to partner with us, not dominate us. He is love, which means that we must freely give Him our heart. We enter into the divine "perichoresis," the circle dance of divine life when we freely respond to His love. But then His love flows out of us into others. Just as God will never dominate us, we must never dominate others.

> ***God gave humans dominion, but not domination.***

Think back to the Garden of Eden. God blessed Adam and Eve and gave them the gracious command to "be fruitful and multiply." He told them to "fill up the earth and subdue it." He then concluded by urging them to "have dominion." (Genesis 1:26-28) But here's the point: God gave humans dominion over the earth, over the fowls of the air, the beasts of the field and the fish of the sea, but never over other people.

God gave humans dominion, but not domination.

We were created in the image of God, which means that we should imitate Him. Since God chose freely to never subjugate humans under His irresistible will, we should do the same. Never should anyone—a man or woman!—dominate another person.

This means that we cannot experience restored divine-human dominion over the earth, which is the point of the Kingdom, until we learn how to govern our relations with each other from love and not power.

King Jesus could have defeated the Roman Empire with overwhelming force. As Jesus said, He could have called twelve legions of angels to annihilate His enemies. The multitudes clamored for Jesus to establish His Kingdom through power. They had no other grid for how the Kingdom should come. In fact, at one point, the people would have made Jesus king over Israel by force:

> *Jesus, perceiving that they were intending to come and take Him by force to make Him king, withdrew again to the mountain by Himself alone." (John 6:15)*

Jesus refused their attempts because His Kingdom was vastly different from what they expected. Jesus' Kingdom would not come through violence. Instead, Jesus willingly submitted to the brutal torture of the cross to demonstrate and effectuate the victory of love over power.

The people—like many today!—simply didn't understand the nature of Christ's Kingdom. The Chief Priests and Sadducees arrested Jesus and turned Him over to the Romans on the charge of treason, on the grounds that He claimed to be a king. As Jesus stood before Pilate, the Roman Procurator asked Jesus specifically if He was indeed a king. Jesus affirmed that it was so, but not like Pilate thought:

> *"My kingdom is not of this world. If My kingdom were of this world, then My servants would be fighting so*

*that I would not be handed over to the Jews; but as it is, My kingdom is not of this realm." (John 18:36)*

Jesus' Kingdom did not derive its existence from within the world order. And His Kingdom would not come through conventional military means. Jesus' Kingdom would only come in the world through regenerated hearts that received the Spirit of Heaven and released Him through love into the world.

No doubt, Pilate was flummoxed. What sort of kingdom is that? A kingdom that does not come through political, military and economic power? A kingdom that does not survive through brute force? That sort of kingdom makes no sense at all to the power brokers of the world.

And it makes no sense to male chauvinists.

Only power makes sense to the power hungry. Power is easier than love. It is so much easier to impose your will on others if you have a superior position than to do the hard work of winning hearts. Ask any parent of a rowdy two-year-old. Barking orders and demanding obedience is much easier than gentle persuasion. The same is true in the workplace, in the neighborhood, in the university, in the Church, anywhere humans gather. Fallen humans would much rather climb the ladder and secure punitive leverage over others so they can impose their will and guarantee getting what they want.

Love requires sacrifice, and sacrifice hurts. People run from pain. So people seek power. But power is a costly shortcut. We may gain the upper hand for now, but, as Jesus put it, those who live by the sword will die by the sword. Power exacts a high cost in the long run. And that's exactly what we've seen with male supremacy. The men got their way for generations, but look at what toxic power structures have done to the world. Look at the wars, the murders, the robberies, the rapes, the evil that has stalked the planet through the lust for power. It's the wrong kingdom.

The Kingdom of God breaks all that. When the Kingdom is unleashed through love, power structures collapse and spirit-systems bow their knee. Love takes time, but when love has had time to work, it is the most powerful force in the world. And I don't mean sappy, sentimental love, though love can be exquisitely sentimental. I don't mean the pretense of love that masquerades as romance. I mean the kind of love that lays down its life for the good of another. I mean that kind of love that looks like a cross raised on a hill for the salvation of all mankind. I mean the kind of love that wins the heart.

All that is why there's such a battle for the human heart. The future of the planet depends on how goes the heart. No wonder we're told to "watch over your heart with all diligence, for from it flow the springs of life." (Proverbs 4:23).

The one who wins human hearts wins the battle for earth. These spiritual kingdoms, both good and evil, are established on earth through people cooperating with God, or with those who oppose Him. Like the parable of the wheat and tares (Matthew 13:24-30), both kingdoms can grow simultaneously in our hearts and in the world around us. No wonder there's such extreme conflict in the world. Yet never fear! The Kingdom of God wins. And it wins through love, not power.

# CHAPTER 4

# THE TOWEL AND BASIN

Somewhere in the middle of this five-year journey into understanding the Kingdom of God, Holy Spirit flashed before my mind two different scenes depicting opposing concepts of the Kingdom. I realized that the two scenes revealed a struggle going on within my spirit to sort out the biblical view of the Kingdom from traditions that had taken deep root in my mind.

Just like I mentioned in Book 1, I needed Nicolas Cage's special *National Treasure* glasses to read the treasure map, to see correctly what was right in front of me. I had been trying to fit the Kingdom of God into my worldly understanding of what any "kingdom" should look like.

When I first heard of the Kingdom of God, I automatically transposed concepts from childhood. You know, the traditional picture of a king sitting on a throne with servants all around him tending to his every wish. Even if the king was benevolent, his government would still be a pyramid-based power structure with all power focused on the top. That's what a kingdom *is*, right? Without realizing it, I corrupted the truth by seeing the Kingdom through faulty filters. I needed new glasses.

What I got was two vivid images flashing like stop-action scenes from a movie. Not entire movies, not even complete scenes. Rather, just two different but powerful images that flashed in my head. Yet a full story line was packed within each image. All in one moment, like an instant download. It is crazy how the Lord can give you a picture with such vivid mental 3-D. A picture is worth a thousand words. In an instant, I began to see the stark differences in the two types of kingdoms.

## *Scene One*

In the first image, the scene looks something like ancient Egypt. A room is filled with a dozen men gathered around a banqueting table. The master of the house is hosting a feast for his friends. They are laughing and talking as they wine-and-dine during what appears to be a festive occasion.

Then, from a darkened side of the room, an emaciated man, wearing nothing but a towel wrapped around his waist, enters carrying a basin of water. You can see the outline of his ribs, and his arms are pencil thin. *He is the master's slave.*

The old slave's back is crisscrossed and glistening with scars from beatings received long ago. His eyes are dark and sunken. Even if you looked deeply into them, it would be hard to find the tiniest flicker of light. At this moment, his face is completely blank, emotionless. He has resigned himself to his position in life, and he is truly in full subjection to his master.

He will smile when his master expects him to smile. He will even laugh at his jokes. But there is no laughter inside him. The smiles and laughter do not flow from his *heart*. Rather, they flow from his *will,* which is now fully yielded to another. He knows what to do on cue, and he is good at going through the motions. He locked away his true self long ago to fit his expected role.

Once his spirit was broken, after he resigned himself to slavery, then winning his master's approval became all that mattered. Now his master no longer needs the whip to get his way, for the slave understands without being told that *his value comes from pleasing the powerful one*. He is beneath his master and must serve him to the best of his weakened ability. The more the slave yields to his master's will, the better it goes for him.

The spiritless skeleton walks across the festive room with the basin of water in his hands. None of the guests notice him as he approaches his master. Then this shell of a man bends down and begins to wash his owner's feet.

Take a deep breath and let the magnitude of that sink in.

### *Scene Two*

Now shake your head and erase that image like an etch-a-sketch. Let's picture a very different scene. This room looks much like the first one, but the setting is first century Israel when Christ walked the earth. Tonight is the feast of the Passover, and Jesus has something special planned. The Passover celebrates Israel's supernatural deliverance from centuries of slavery in Egypt. *It is the feast of freedom!*

Here in the upper room, Jesus gathers His twelve disciples around a banqueting table as He hosts the Passover Seder. By this time, Jesus has walked closely with these men for three and a half years. They know Him well. They have personally experienced His love, His miracles and His teachings. There is no doubt they comprehend how amazing and powerful this Man truly is. He even raised the dead! By now, they grasp the fact that He is their long-awaited Messiah. He is indeed their Rabbi, their Lord—*their Master*.

Here in this room filled with a dozen men gathered around a banqueting table, our Master hosts a feast for his friends. They laugh and talk as they wine-and-dine during this festive occasion. As the host, Jesus leads them through the traditional Seder ceremony.

Then the Master does something totally unexpected, something out of the norm for this occasion. He gets up and removes His marvelous robe. It's the same robe that Roman soldiers will cast lots for tomorrow. Jesus slowly and purposefully wraps a towel around His waist. While the disciples watch in puzzled curiosity, He fills a basin with water. This amazing Man, filled with strength and power, walks across the festive room. The Master bends down to wash the disciples' dusty feet.

The room falls silent. All laughter stops. When Jesus reaches Peter, the last in line, the burly fisherman protests indignantly. How can the Master serve him like a slave? No way! But Jesus, as an act of free will, from a position of strength and honor, chooses freely to do so. He is not being forced. He was not even asked. Jesus serves from His heart. And on the eve of His execution, He teaches his disciples *how to live and how to lead as free men*.

## *Same Act, Different Kingdoms*

Two very different scenes. Yet in each scene a man with a towel and a basin bends down to wash the feet of another. Two men, two basins. But each man models vastly different kingdoms. The first one is the kingdom of darkness built on dehumanizing power. The second one is the Kingdom of Light built on affirming love. Both kingdoms exercise power, but the purpose of power is profoundly different.

The first is a story of human domination and subjection. It is a picture of the dark kingdom that seeks to dominate and control others, as the strong force their will upon the weak. It robs human beings of their true identity as the beloved apple of their Creator's eye. It places them in the bondage of slavery where they have no choice and where bully-cowards rule.

The kingdom of darkness persuades people to agree with the lie that they are lesser in worth and therefore must serve others from a place of weakness. First, the dark kingdom robs them of their identity; then, their strength; and finally, their freedom.

The second scene is a story of honor and dignity. It is a story of a valiant, powerful person who voluntarily gives of Himself to serve others. As an independent act of His own free will, He serves from a position of strength. Jesus teaches by demonstration what honor, servanthood and freedom look like in the Kingdom of God where kings rule nobly.

Human subjection and domination are the essence of the dark kingdom. Slavery demands that you yield your will to another. It is the antithesis of freedom and the antithesis of love.

> ***Human subjection and domination are the essence of the dark kingdom.***

Freedom and voluntary service are the essence of the Kingdom of Light. The second scene is beautiful; it's powerful —*and it is completely voluntary*. It is important to understand that these two kingdoms are not just different, they are diametrically opposed to one another. They are at war with each other. They cannot peacefully co-exist. It is the clash of kingdoms.

In both cases, one man with a towel and basin bend down to wash the feet of another. How can the exact same act demonstrate two clashing kingdoms? Both are serving, but one serves willingly with love from the heart. The other serves under compulsion with fear from habit. One serves to help another. One serves to survive.

Do you see how this impacts male-female relations? If Christ has made both male and female one, then how can men justify forcing women to serve? How can they excuse imposing subjugation on women made in the image of God? There is no way that Christ's Kingdom can ever operate from the demand, "Hey, you! Wash my feet!" Or get my supper. Or bring me some tea. Or wash those dishes. Or whatever men demand.

The strongest command in Scripture vis-a-vis men and women is that men love their wives as Christ loves the Church *and gave Himself for it.* (Ephesians 5) The most powerful expression of Kingdom manhood is the love displayed at the cross. Jesus, after willingly washing His disciples' feet, led the way, the way that we all must follow, down the *Via Dolorosa* to Golgotha. And there He demonstrated the unstoppable power of self-sacrificing love.

This is the love that restructures and reconstitutes human society. When this kind of selfless love gets loose in the world, demons flee in terror. Tyrants roar in dismay as their thrones topple into dust. Abusers shrivel and snivel in cowardice and fear. The oppressed rise up from the ashes like the phoenix and soar in freedom. The beauty of creation is rediscovered and darkness recedes into fading shadow as the light of Christ rises like the sun.

## *Back to the Heart*

It all comes back to the heart. The man in the first story washed feet from a broken and resentful heart. The second man, Jesus the Christ, washed feet from a joyful, willing heart. No matter how complicated our theology gets, and no matter how convoluted our world gets, the truth remains simple:

*It all comes back to the heart!*

Free men live out of their heart. Slaves do what they are told. Anytime you choose to submit to someone else, or any time you choose to serve, ask yourself why you are doing it. It doesn't matter if you are male or female, when you submit to someone else, check to see what's going on in your heart. Do you feel like you "have-to"? Or do you "get-to"? Are you going through the motions like a powerless slave who has no choice? Or are you choosing to serve from a place of strength and honor? Can you see how significant the answers to those questions can be?

This is one reason that Jesus taught His disciples to turn the other cheek, go the extra mile and give away more than asked. (Matthew 5:38-42) When someone slaps you on the cheek, they are operating from power. But when you turn the other cheek back to them, you overcome power with love. You actually strip them of their power to control you. Your willingness to suffer wrong actually breaks their domination. How can someone take from me what I willingly give? This is what Jesus did on the cross, and when we imitate Him, we unleash Kingdom love into a power-crazed world.

When Jesus washed the disciples' feet, He gave them a pattern, a template, for how life should be done. He taught them to humble themselves as servants to one another. Jesus taught them *mutual submission*. Jesus taught them that Kingdom power flows from love freely given. In the Kingdom, no one ever compels someone to wash his or her feet. Rather, each one gladly offers to wash another's.

Jesus made loving service the primary pattern of life in the Kingdom. Look at how John described the lesson to be learned:

> *So when He had washed their feet, and taken His garments and reclined at the table again, He said to them, "Do you know what I have done to you? You call Me*

> *Teacher and Lord; and you are right, for so I am. If I then, the Lord and the Teacher, washed your feet, you also ought to wash one another's feet. For I gave you an example that you also should do as I did to you.* (John 13:12–15)

Catch the key phrase: "Do you know what I have done to you?" Do you get it? Do you understand the significance of what Jesus did? So then, apply that lesson to male and female relations. Did Jesus intend for this story to apply only to men serving each other? Or to only women serving men? I think not. Jesus meant that everyone in the Kingdom, including men and women, would serve each other out of mutual submission. The prevailing order of male supremacy that has dominated human history is not from the Kingdom of God. It is the wrong kingdom.

# CHAPTER 5

# THERE WERE TWO TREES IN THE GARDEN

As I journeyed further on my Kingdom odyssey, abrupt questions kept popping up out of nowhere. Each question carried a powerful, new insight on the Kingdom that deepened my awareness of how wrong male or female supremacy really is, how much dominance over others is the *wrong kingdom*. One of those out-of-nowhere questions took me back to the Garden of Eden.

Why were there two trees in the middle of the garden?

Smack dab in the middle of God's perfect paradise, He placed two trees, the "*Tree of Life*" and the "*Tree of the Knowledge of Good and Evil*." (Genesis 2:9)

As you may know, the second tree was forbidden:

> *The Lord God commanded the man, saying, "From any tree of the garden you may eat freely; but from the tree of the knowledge of good and evil you shall not eat, for in the day that you eat from it you will surely die." (Genesis 2:16–17)*

If God did not want Adam and Eve to eat from the forbidden tree, then why did He put it there? Or why didn't He block their access to it? Geez, He could have at least built a wall or a fence! After all, He is God—large and in charge. *God could have easily created a garden where humans had no choice but to remain safe.* But He did not. He created a world with options. He created a world with risk. Why?

There had to be two trees in the garden because *love always offers a choice.* If you are not given a choice, you are not free. If you are not free, you cannot love.

## *Love Always Offers A Choice*

Love has to flow freely from the heart. For love to be true, it cannot be coerced. You cannot *make* someone love you. As Paul said in 1 Corinthians 13, love never demands its own way.

The Kingdom of God works from love because God *is* love. The nature of the Kingdom is defined by the King. There are three signature phrases in Scripture that describe who God is essentially and existentially.

(1) God is *one*. He exists eternally as triune union-in-communion. Father, Son and Spirit—three-in-one, unity-in-diversity. This sort of oneness underlies all created reality, insomuch that all things find their purpose only when they find their unity-in-diversity with all other created things. Talk about the ultimate "unified theory of everything"!

(2) God is *holy*. God exists in complete, unified transcendence. The "holiness" of God is the "whole-i-ness of God. As Paul Ellis puts it, "Holiness means perfection in the sense of completion."[1] God is whole, without brokenness and fragmentation.

(3) God is *love*. Love is not an attribute of God, a feeling that He may or may not experience depending on how the day goes. God *is* love, essentially and existentially. Love is not what God does—love is who God is. "God is love, and the one who abides in love abides in God, and God abides in him" (1 John 4:16).

Since God *is* love, divine power flows from love. God's power is an expression of His love. God will never impose His

---

[1] https://escapetoreality.org/2012/05/23/what-is-holiness/

will because His will is an expression of His love. Love cannot be forced; thus, God works out His will in the world by pouring out His love upon us. And the love of God is so real, so strong, so transformative, that those who yield to His love respond with love. Love begets love.

This is how a sovereign God guarantees His purpose: He loves so deeply and powerfully that His love liberates the enslaved human will and restores people back to the God-loving creatures they were originally created to be.

On the other hand, the only way satan can enslave humans is to get them to doubt God's love, to question God's goodness, His desire for what's best for us. As Paul said, "Faith works by love" (Galatians 5:6). So the best way to undermine faith and produce unbelief is to make people doubt the love of God.

> ***Though God is sovereign, He does not force us to do His will.***

Contrary to popular opinion, even though God is sovereign, He does not force us to do His will. He does not violate the nature of love—ever![2] Love never controls or manipulates. It does not dominate or force.

This is where I got tripped up in my understanding. I used to believe we had to do what God wanted or He wouldn't love us. In fact, I would read the scriptures, particularly the Old Testament, as if God was a dictator who would punish those who disobeyed Him. I saw Him through a faulty filter. That is not who He is or how He exercises His power and authority. He is love, and that's not how love acts. He may use force to protect, but never for selfish gain.

---

[2] 1 Corinthians 13: These characteristics of love describe God, for God is love.

God's power is always an expression of His love.

## *Freedom*

Love requires freedom. And freedom is always the natural by-product of love. You simply cannot have one without the other. The Apostle Paul tells us that we were set free *for* freedom. Freed to be free.

> *It was for freedom that Christ set us free; therefore keep standing firm and do not be subject again to a yoke of slavery. (Galatians 5:1)*

The yoke of slavery means you feel you have no choice, and you are doing things because you "have-to" not because you "get-to." Our freedom is so important to God that Jesus died to protect it.

Of course, understanding freedom requires a good definition of freedom. Too many mis-define freedom and end up with a pseudo-freedom, which is another way of saying "slavery." So here's a good definition of freedom:

Freedom is the liberty to choose what allows you to be everything you were originally created to be.

Freedom is not "free to do whatever you want." No, freedom is "free to be who you were created to be." The reason that distinction matters is because sin distorts our desires, and if we see freedom as the liberty to do whatever we want, our "freedom" will become slavery to impulses that prevent us from full self-actualization in Christ. We will become a slave to our lusts.

Here's how Peter put it:

> *For speaking out arrogant words of vanity they entice by fleshly desires, by sensuality, those who barely escape from the ones who live in error, promising them freedom while they themselves are slaves of corruption; for by what*

*a man is overcome, by this he is enslaved. (2 Peter 2:18–19)*

When we are saved, our heart is regenerated by the Holy Spirit. We, who were dead, come alive in Christ. In that moment, our will is liberated. We are set free to desire what God originally created us to be. That's true freedom.

If you release an eagle from captivity, the majestic bird will soar to the heavens. That's what it was created to do. But if you've trained that eagle to scratch for worms in a chicken coop, and if, when you release it, it keeps on scratching the ground because *that's what you've trained it to want*, that eagle is not yet free even though it's doing exactly what it wants to do. Its wants are all jacked up. The eagle is not free until it becomes free to be what it was created to be.

The same is true for you and me. True freedom is "free to be."

In fact, true freedom often means doing *what you do not want to do* in order to become *what you were meant to be*. Ask the bodybuilder. Ask the athlete. Ask the musician. Ask the business owner. Ask the parent, for crying out loud.

Are there times that you do things you do not want to do in order to achieve things that you deeply long to achieve?

The answer is a solid "yes." Always.

Being takes precedence over doing. In fact, *doing* must flow out of *being* or we become untrue to who really are. Those who focus on *doing* rather than *being* become hypocrites, obsessed with pretense and appearance. They become performance-driven perfectionists.

Real freedom is rooted in knowing who you are. Identity over performance. And that's why love and freedom are so closely intertwined: only real love values who we truly are. False love demands performance. True love seeks integrity.

Integrity is *wholeness*. Wholeness is *oneness, holiness* and *love* all wrapped up together. And that is God.

When you know who you are, identity redefines what you want. You will do what you don't want in the short-term to get what you *do* want in the long-term. And that's perfectly consistent with true freedom.

Think about it now. You often do what you don't want to do in order to be what you want to be. As adults, we all pay rent or mortgage payments, property taxes and utilities because we want to be homeowners. We make these payments whether we want to or not. If we don't pay, we don't get to stay.

Want that car? Buy it in cash or pay the payments. Either way, you'll have to do what you don't want to do—fork over the *dinero*—in order to get something greater that you *do* want.

> ***You often do what you don't want to do in order to be what you want to be.***

And when you grasp the value of short-term self-denial to achieve long-term self-actualization, you see even the things you don't really want to do transformed into a "get-to" opportunity rather than a "have-to" obligation. This is how truly free people can go through unpleasant, undesirable circumstances with a gratitude-attitude. This is how truly free people reject short-term self-gratification as pseudo-freedom, a false freedom that forfeits destiny and enslaves the soul.

It's all a matter of the heart. Our attitude totally shifts when we see the long view of a life lived in love. We pay those house payments and utilities with a grateful heart, truly thankful that we have a place to stay. We are thankful for a community that uses our taxes for schools, roads, police and fire departments. Because we are free to live with a "get-to" spirit, we refuse to live each day frustrated and paying our share begrudgingly.

It's all a matter of the heart. Picture parents who constantly complain about how much it costs to have their kids in sports and activities outside of school. They whine about the amount of time they spend running them around. These parents feel like they never have anything left for themselves, no money, no time, no energy. For whatever reason, they still do it all, but only because they feel like they "have to."

Now picture different parents who lost their kids in a tragic accident. What would they give to have the opportunity to take their kids to football practice or to pay for their uniforms? They would gladly give their money, time and energy. In fact, they would probably give up everything for the privilege of doing those simple everyday things with their children again. For them, it would be a "get-to," not a "have-to."

We don't have to suffer loss to serve from a place of gratitude. We can guard our hearts and manage our attitudes. We can embrace love and serve others. Or we can be self-centered and self-serving. The choice is ours. Obviously, how we choose impacts those around us because we are wired together in community. How others choose impacts us as well.

How do we guard our hearts or manage our attitudes? By staying connected with the Holy Spirit who lives inside us! God is love. He is joy. He is peace. He has everything we need, so we can draw from Him. We can rely on His strength and His goodness. Sounds simple, yes? It is. May not always be easy in the moment of fear or frustration, but it is simple. He is always available.

Love always offers a choice.

When God created a perfect world, before sin invaded paradise, God gave humans a choice. Do you see that? The choice existed before the Fall. The choice was "good," as was everything God created. Humans were formed in a perfect environment of love, and there were two trees in that perfect love environment. Choice! It's essential to love.

This is what the Kingdom is like. The Kingdom creates an environment of love that offers choice to ensure genuine freedom. Love does not force anyone to do anything. That's what Kingdom freedom is like.

Remember, we're still talking about how understanding the Kingdom shifts our view of male and female relations. God, the Supreme Being of the universe, created a world of choice where love flourished through the freedom of image-bearing males and females. There was no manipulation or control in the garden. All that came after sin entered the world. There was no male supremacy—or female supremacy. Love reigned. Choice was available. People were free to be who they were created to be by freely choosing to eat from the Tree of Life.

Then humans, through free choice, made the decision to believe a lie and disobey the Father. Sin came and violence entered the world. For more than four thousand long years, the world was wracked by violence and fear. But Jesus came to restore creation back to its original design—*love, freedom and choice!* Jesus came to liberate the human will so that we could again freely choose life, so that we could freely choose actions that actualize our destiny.

Now that we are born again into the Kingdom, we choose freely to obey the will of the Father. We choose to live in a "get-to" frame of mind. We choose gratitude over entitlement. We choose life over death. That's the Kingdom.

## *Family Matters*

If we were created for love, then why do we gravitate toward power? No doubt it is because we are born unregenerate and under the power of sin. But there's another layer to why we inherently and inevitably grasp for power: our *family of origin*.

We all first learned about love from our family. And most of us learned it wrong. While most of us experienced *true* love, yet it was still *imperfect* love, love alloyed with power. I think it would be safe to say that for many of us, family life was structured around power and control rather than love and freedom. Many of us have difficulty understanding how love works in the family of God because we have never seen it modeled in our own family life. Most of us grew up in households that were constantly torn by power struggles between mom and dad, parents and kids, brothers and sisters. Most choices were simply the compromises necessary to maintain a fragile, false peace.

This is especially true if you were reared in a traditional family where dad was the supreme authority and all of life was ordered around him. In some cultures, the head of the family having all the power is considered normal and even good. Generations of tradition trains the family that it is the father's God-given right to rule and that bad things will happen if the subordinates do not obey.

Often, tyrannical fathers force their will on the younger, weaker members. A culture akin to slavery is fostered in the home. Selfish, authoritarian husbands and parents create dysfunctional families, who in turn repeat the patterns they were raised in. They pass on a culture founded on selfishness, fear and control rather than a culture founded on love, honor, and freedom.

Or maybe your family life was matriarchal, and mom dominated dad and everyone else in the house. Maybe neither—maybe your home operated on a sliding scale somewhere between extreme patriarchy and extreme matriarchy. However it may have been for you, most of us grew up in a home where power was the root motivation. The Kingdom is exactly the opposite. Love is the root motivation.

No wonder we have trouble understanding how the Kingdom works. We were all raised in broken households that were molded to one degree or another by the power systems of the world. We attended schools defined by power. We took recess on playgrounds defined by power. We attended summer camps organized around power. We went to college and joined sororities or fraternities based on human supremacy of one type or another. We showed up on our first day at work and quickly learned where we fit in the hierarchy of power. It's all about climbing another rung on the ladder of power.

Then we go to church and it's the same: religious power structures that mirror the systems of the world.

All this has everything to do with how we view male and female relations in the world. The power-based systems of the world have worked their way into all human relations—marriage, parenting, work and religion—and there's no place where it's been more apparent than the millennia-long oppression of women.

Can you see how the subordination of women cannot fit in the Kingdom of God? Can you see how different the culture of God's Kingdom is from the worldly and religious atmospheres that are permeated with dominance and demand obedience?

If you believe you are powerless, you will wait for someone else to tell you what to do. You will be totally unable to accept responsibility for becoming everything you were created to be. You will not take dominion over the darkness in your own life. Kingdom advance will stall dead still in your life. You will feel powerless and under the domination of others. God hates that slavery, and Jesus came to break it, to empower you with the ultimate empowerment —the love of God!

Sadly enough, the false power structures of the world are religious in origin. Theologians, scholars and Bible teachers have presented a false view of God's sovereignty for years and shaped our thinking, which shaped our culture. Many theologians hold the idea that God controls everything, so they unwittingly created a religious culture with powerless believers. If "God is in control," then whatever He wants will inevitably happen. This creates a view of God that is demanding and controlling.

***If you believe you are powerless, you will wait for someone else to tell you what to do.***

The next step is an easy one: if God leads with total control, then men should too. Sort of like "the divine right of kings" that was such a big deal in the Middle Ages. Kings justified their dictatorial control of nations based on the example of God's sovereignty over the world.

This even leads to a "theodicy" (theology of divine justice) that blames God for evil. If God is totally in control, then He's controlling the bad stuff too. For example, when a child dies tragically, we may hear at the funeral how God must have wanted them in Heaven. Like it was by God's permission that the child died—or worse, that God took the child on purpose. That is a dysfunctional, perverted view of God's sovereignty.

If a human parent allowed his or her child to die when he or she had the power to rescue the child, that parent would go to jail for neglect and child abuse. If the parent took his or her child's life on purpose, he or she would go to prison for murder. Then why do we think it's okay for God to do the same? Because we have twisted views of God's sovereignty.

Our God is a good, good Father. He would never harm us. He would never sin against His own kids. Too often we believe that God perpetrates these evil acts, and then we justify Him by sayings things like, "God's ways are not our ways." These lies about Him have been woven into the fabric of our society. They are commonly believed and widespread.

Our view of God's sovereignty is colored by our family experience. Of course, God, like any good parent, expects obedience. But obedience in the Kingdom is never about control. It's always about discipline, training us to live in wisdom. Obedience is designed to guide us until we can internalize wisdom and freely choose behavior that aligns with our destiny and purpose. And even if we choose disobedience, our Heavenly Father does not *force* us to obey. He lets us choose folly, then helps us clean up the inevitable mess folly makes.

## *Partnering With God*

How we view the sovereignty of God is a big deal. The father of lies gains tremendous advantage when Christians unknowingly twist the truth. Many believe that since God is in control (which He is), then He is micromanaging their lives (which He is not). If God were orchestrating every detail, humans would be powerless to affect the outcome. We would all be nothing more than puppets on a string.

The enemy loves it when we believe the lie that everything that happens is God's will being done. If everything that happens is God's will, then why fight the devil at all? Why pray? Why fast? Why prophesy different outcomes? This false view of God's sovereignty trains people to be fatalistic, helpless pawns in the hands of remorseless fate. And it reduces us all to bitter cynics.

That is often how our heart interprets life's hardships. We believe that God allowed darkness into our life, that He personally approved the pain or the sickness. If we believe that our suffering is God's will, we will not go deep to fully fight against it. We may go through the motions of resistance —like going to see a doctor when we get sick, for example— but we will not truly fight evil from the bottom of our heart.

Further, the belief system that God is micromanaging every detail fails to consider our role and responsibility in the world. It fails to take responsibility for our part in the problem and our part in the solution. Do not forget that God gave us dominion over this world. God is completely sovereign, and He owns it all. However, He put humans in charge of the earth. That was our mandate at creation.

When we understand it is God's will for us to reign with Him, then many of the Bible stories start to make more sense. It is neither "all on God" nor "all on us." Dominion is a partnership. God chose not to do anything on the earth except through people. Even though He is certainly able, He does not want to force His will. He wants to partner with His family.

Love always offers choices.

That's why we pray. We partner with God to declare and decree His will on the earth through our voluntary cooperation and agreement. He wants to move through us, not on us.

Remember the story of Elijah and the drought? (1 Kings 17-18) God refused to bring rain on the earth unless Elijah prayed for it because He wanted man's agreement. The New Testament looks back at this same story to demonstrate the power of our prayers:

> *Elijah was a man with a nature like ours, and he prayed earnestly that it would not rain, and it did not rain on the earth for three years and six months. Then he prayed again, and the sky poured rain and the earth produced its fruit. (James 5:17-18)*

We become powerless when we believe God is micromanaging the universe without our participation. We develop a victim mentality and unwittingly allow the enemy to wage war against our thinking. Our actions always reflect our true beliefs. We sit back like a powerless slave and let the kingdom of darkness rule the earth because we fail to understand who we are in the Kingdom.

**_Love always offers choices._**

Can you imagine a world where freedom and love are at the core of its culture? Where mutual, reciprocal honor and submission would purposefully yield, one to another? That's pretty hard to imagine. It seems more like a fairy tale, especially considering when one of the partners—God!—is so much more powerful than the others. But our majestic God, worthy of worship and all praise, voluntarily wants to partner with mankind. Why? *Because God is love, and love always offers choices.*

The family of God is not a dysfunctional family with a dictator or tyrant leading his subjects. Rather, it is a healthy family where the rules of relationship require mutual, reciprocal honor and mutual, reciprocal submission. It is how the Kingdom of love works.

Since God is love, and God is triune, then love exists in relationship. Love is how God the Father, the Son and the Holy Spirit interact with one another. There's that perichoresis again.

Sometimes our theology gets messed up, and we try to force a hierarchical, domineering mindset into the Trinity. But that is not biblically based. (Ontological hierarchy within the Trinity was the heresy of "subordinationism" that was so firmly rejected by the Early Church.) For example, Jesus voluntarily yielded His will to the Father when it came to the cross. No one forced Him. He said, "No one has taken [my life] away from Me, but I lay it down on My own initiative" (John 10:18). Jesus' decision to lay down His life was motivated only by love, not force.

Sadly, I have heard sermons which taught that since God is sovereign, and since the plan of salvation was set from the foundation of the world, then Jesus actually had no choice but to go to the cross.

Many use Jesus' obedience to the Father as a prime example of submission to absolute sovereignty. That would make sense if Jesus had not declared exactly the opposite—Jesus said that He laid down His life freely, on His own initiative. In the Garden when Jesus was sweating blood, He said,

> *"Father, if You are willing, remove this cup from Me; yet not My will, but Yours be done." (Luke 22:42)*

Jesus yielded His will voluntarily. The Father would have sent help if Jesus had asked:

*"Or do you think that I cannot appeal to My Father, and He will at once put at My disposal more than twelve legions of angels?" (Matthew 26:53)*

Jesus was not forced onto the cross. Nor was He forced to stay there. He acted out of love, not out of compulsion.

*Love always offers choices.*

God is indeed sovereign. He knows the end from the beginning, and He can turn the hearts of kings when He chooses. He created this world with His Word, and He holds the entire universe in the palm of His hands. God could force us do His will if He wanted, but He does not want to. He wants us to know His love.

God, in His sovereignty, chose to invest free will within us, and He often goes to great lengths to protect it—even limiting His own will. Why would the Almighty God ever yield His will to ours? Because that is what love does. He loves us and wants to create an environment of freedom and honor.

God is *not* looking for slaves to obey Him. That approach to power is the epitome of the wrong kingdom. Nor does our Heavenly Father want us to remain like toddlers in our relationship with Him, where He can rightfully boss us around like a controlling parent. Father God is looking for a much deeper and more meaningful relationship. He is raising up a Kingdom family. He loves for His mature sons and daughters to partner with Him to take over the family business, which is establishing His Kingdom here on earth.

That's what the Father wanted at the beginning when He installed Adam and Eve in the garden. In order for the first humans to grow into the maturity of real divine-human partnership, they had to face a real choice—and face the consequences of their free decision. God could not make the choice for them. The only way humans can bear the image and share the glory of God is to function out of true love, and true love requires free choice.

Love always offers choices.

And that's why God placed two trees in the garden.

# CHAPTER 6

## THE KINGDOM IS NOT A PYRAMID SCHEME!

If Jesus showed up on earth and established His Kingdom, what would it look like? (Spoiler Alert! Jesus *did* show up on earth and establish His Kingdom—that's what He's doing through you and me.)

But seriously, what would the Kingdom look like? Would it look like Buckingham Palace, Windsor Castle or one of the oil-rich kingdoms of the Middle East? What would it look like?

Remember, I told you earlier that my childhood view of kings and kingdoms deeply affected my concept of the Kingdom of God. I inherited a "top-down" view of kingliness that made me automatically think that God's Kingdom was like that.

Then I learned that freedom lies at the heart of Christ's Kingdom. It is a love-centered Kingdom that treasures free choice over forced compliance. A Kingdom that celebrates people even in their weakness and mistakes. A Kingdom that honors people for who they will be, not criticizes them for who they are. God is perfect, but He's not a perfectionist.

But there was always one thing that bothered me about all this freedom stuff: what do you do when freedom goes bad, just like it did in Eden? If freedom lies at the core of Kingdom culture, how do you govern a free people? Most importantly, how do we ensure that the purposes of God get done? If humans are free, can they theoretically choose not to do God's will *forever* and thus frustrate and flummox the

Most High? Isn't God taking quite a risk giving treacherous humans the right to choose?

Of course, I was only one person in a long line of people trying to sort out the balance between divine sovereignty and human free will. But I really wrestled with this. And it was quite practical to me. It had to do with how we govern relationships in the real world, particularly in the Church where I was facing all these questions for the first time.

For so long the "freedom vs. control" conundrum felt like an unsolvable mystery to me. If people could do whatever they want, chaos and selfishness would rule the day, wouldn't it? How could we ensure fairness if we emphasized freedom? (That's the argument lying at the heart of the socialism vs. capitalism debate.)

> ***Religion panics at the idea of people being free.***

Briefly, just to keep from dragging you through years of pondering with me, I ended up settling rather carefully but confidently on the idea expressed above that God's love is powerful enough to influence the hearts of people to freely choose the right thing without force.

Religion doesn't like this. Religion panics at the idea of people being free. Religion wants control over people because it fears failure and being considered imperfect by others. Religion is rooted in pride, which is the deep, existential need to be affirmed as superior by others. Free people tend to embarrass the control freaks among us.

So religion creates endless rules of conduct that will guarantee "righteous" outcomes and preserve an unsullied reputation. Religion is more worried about image than reality, more about reputation than character.

But does religion work? Does it produce more perfect people? Does religion do a better job managing people? No, it does not. The power structures of religion do not produce righteousness. They produce only *self-righteousness*.

From my observation, there is one primary reason for this: the structure is wrong. Religion, and every other false kingdom, architects a "top-down" structure that gains power by oppressing people. Again, this is rooted in pride, the need to be seen as superior. One of the best examples of a "wrong-structured kingdom" is Babel where humans attempted to ascend the heavens by building a tower *up to the top*.

This wrong structure is the "power structure" that we spoke about earlier. "Power" in its corrupt form is the attempt to control others to ensure we get what we want. Power in its most venal form is witchcraft. This "power-grab" is rooted in the primal nature of humans, the need to organize hierarchically and establish worth based on proximity to power. Humans experience this whenever they gather in groups, from playgrounds to boardrooms. Jordan Peterson calls it "lobster brain," the primal urge to arrange ourselves in ranks of dominance and sub-dominance. The Bible just calls it pride.

But the impulse to achieve dominance over other humans is a result of the Fall. It is not how God made the world. The lust for predominance flows from an alternative kingdom, the kingdom of darkness that gains power over humans when they willingly choose to believe a lie.

And this is why religion ultimately cannot produce righteousness—its root is pride. And pride always "goes before a fall" as humans are unable to sustain the pretense for long. Organizations, communities, families and any other group of people that organizes their structure along these lines will eventually produce deep corruption.

Humans were not created to be controlled, and given enough time they will revert to hypocrisy and secret rebellion against the powers-that-be. And, by this means, *control* will produce *chaos,* exactly the opposite of what it sought. Every action produces a reaction. The rich irony is that those who oppose freedom in order to impose order always end up producing the disorder they were trying to prevent.

Religious power-grabs are particularly dangerous. And that's also ironic because the goal of religion at its best is to mediate the power and presence of God to the world. Yet, again and again, we see powerful religious figures fall into disgrace and bring shame on the name of Jesus. As they rise to "the top," they often fall prey to the same temptations those without God do—like pride, greed and sexual immorality. Throughout Church history, many great leaders with miraculous ministries started out well but ended up off track. Why? Power corrupts.

But hold on a second. Aren't leaders—especially Spirit-empowered leaders—supposed to be powerful? Didn't Jesus tell the disciples to wait in Jerusalem until they were "clothed with power from on high"? Yes, they are. And, yes, He did.

So what is the problem?

The problem is where the power comes from. Jesus told His disciples to be "clothed with power from on high"—from heaven. Powerful leaders, even religious leaders, often switch the source of power from relationship with God to relationship with people. Their source becomes the people-power systems around them. They begin to derive their power from the world's energy sources like money, popularity, fame, publicity, influence—all sources rooted in human supremacy, contracted from a infectious "dog-eat-dog" world.

The reason these great leaders get off track is because their power isn't flowing from the right kingdom. These leaders unconsciously end up building little kingdoms for themselves that are quite different from the one King Jesus modeled. Following the example of the world, these leaders usually elevate one powerful person (or a small group of powerful people) at the top while everyone else under them remains powerless.

Jesus was powerful, for sure. But he never arrogated power to himself at the top while pressing those under Him into subservient roles. Jesus' goal was that His disciples would do "greater things" than He did. Jesus' modeled and mediated power so that His disciples would gain power and ability from Him. Jesus was never interested in protecting His prerogatives while making sure the underlings never got above themselves.

Those of you sitting on the front row and paying close attention can see clearly where this is going: when the Kingdom comes, male and female relations are radically transformed in the family, Church and society.

## *Why Isn't Christianity Changing the World?*

So why do the followers of Jesus seem to build kingdoms that are so diametrically opposed to His? How does that happen? It happens because Christians often build with the same basic governmental and hierarchical structures as the world. We use the wrong model.

Think about the sheer number of Christians world-wide—over two billion people. Here in America, almost three-quarters of the population identify with a Christian faith (forty-nine percent Protestant, twenty-three percent Catholic, two percent Mormon).[1] With that being the case, why does it seem that Christians have so little influence in the "real world," in what many call "the mountains" of society? Why are all the realms of societal influence dominated by the godless?

Think about the following spheres:

- Business
- Government
- Education
- Science and technology
- Arts and entertainment
- News and media
- Family
- Health and medicine
- Religion and spirituality

How many of these spheres would you say truly operate under the dominion of humans in partnership with heaven? Has the Kingdom come significantly in any of them? Maybe some would say that family and religion have been widely influenced by the Kingdom, but I'm not so sure. So much religion is fettered by tradition, and the family is in an infamous mess. So I'm not sure we can claim much success in either one.

> ***You cannot take the culture of God's Kingdom, put it into the wrong structure, and still expect it to flourish.***

Should we think that it is God's will that all these spheres be more influenced by the dark side than by the Kingdom of Light? Of course not! So how can Christians be

[1] https://news.gallup.com/poll/224642/2017-update-americans-religion.aspx

so non-influential when we claim to know the mighty power and sovereignty of God? How can darkness prevail so completely when a great majority of our population confesses Christ as King, as Lord and Savior?

The answer is quite simple—and quite profound:

*You cannot implant the culture of God's Kingdom in the wrong structure and still expect it to flourish.*

That would be like taking a fish out of water and expecting it to swim. It's just not going to happen. The Kingdom simply cannot flourish using the wrong system.

Get this now. This is the key that unlocks the mystery to ruling and reigning with Christ. The Kingdom of God on earth does not have the typical pyramid-style organizational structure that we are so familiar with. Nor should Christian families. Or churches. Or businesses. This Kingdom refuses to hierarchalize and subdue people, not just because it is a "spiritual" Kingdom without geographic boundaries, but also because the Kingdom reflects the heart of its King.

## *The Pyramid Structure*

Picture a pyramid. A triangular structure, narrow at the top and wide at the bottom. That's how most social systems are organized, and that's what we see modeled around us from early childhood on. So, naturally, we assume that's how God's Kingdom should be structured. When that's all you know, that's all you expect. Add to that our common perceptions of "top down" kingdoms throughout history, and it's no wonder we expect God's Kingdom to look just like that.

Within a pyramid kingdom, the king reigns at the top of the pyramid. The original king of the hill! Those downline from the king both serve those above them and rule those below. Everyone is "under" and "over." Except the king—he's over everyone and serves no one. Everyone's under the king.

This pyramid form of human hierarchy is a sort of social contract that we all accept and abide by for the most part. This is true whether you are talking about a government, a business, a church and even a family. In fact, the patriarchal family is doubtless the oldest form of pyramid government in the world—the father rules as the king.

The pyramid mindset creates a natural hierarchy. Within this kind of organizational structure, people's value and significance comes from how close to the top they can get. We measure ourselves based on where we are on the ladder: "Another rung higher, and I'll finally achieve significance! At least, I'll be better than that other guy."

Then, eventually, within every pyramid, two general groups of people form. Those who strive to be as close to the top as they can and those who believe they are powerless to move up. Who you hang out with matters, so naturally we divide. The pyramid-style environment creates a competition culture that breeds jealousy, envy and strife. As James said, "For where jealousy and selfish ambition exist, there is disorder and every evil thing" (James 3:16). The pyramid promotes pride, greed and selfishness. It fosters human domination and corruption.

The fact that God's Kingdom could look like this—supposed to be heaven, but more like hell!—was one of the most difficult realities for me to face. I could see where the world would operate like this, but the Church? And yet it did. I had to wrestle for a while with what I saw around me in the Church.

But then I also had to grapple with the heartbreaking reality that the Church was powerless to influence the world as long as it operated by the world's standards and systems. As one unbelieving critic put it:

> I am not religious, so it is not my place to dictate to Christians what they should and should not believe. Still, if someone has a faith worth following, I feel that their beliefs should make me feel uncomfortable for not doing so. If they share ninety percent of my lifestyle and values, then there is nothing especially inspiring about them. Instead of making me want to become more like them, it looks very much as if they want to become more like me.[2]

Is that not heartbreaking? It seems sometimes that outsiders see more clearly why the Church has so little influence in the world. It's hard to influence what you imitate. As long as we order our Christian society around the pyramid system, we can expect to produce the same sinful culture.

One of the things I learned as I studied and prayed through the lack of Christian influence in the world was that it's not just that we have bad people at the helm—it's that we have the wrong sort of helm. It does us no good whatsoever to ferret out corrupt leaders and replace them with good people because the system soon corrupts the latest good people. The way we organize people and distribute power is what must change. The system is the problem.

Jesus declared that He would build His Church upon the rock. But His building program keeps getting held up by people trying to redesign His Church according to the wrong blueprint. We look around us and see the "success" of the world and its systems. We lust for the fame and fortune that brings quick approbation and thunderous applause. We crave the praise of men, so we try to reengineer the Church after the world's values.

---

[2] https://spectator.us/sad-irony-celebrity-pastors-carl-lentz-hillsong/

When success is measured by the world's metrics, the pyramid system is the most efficient way to gain success. It's the best way to manage people and distribute power. Ask the builders of Babel. Get people in their slot and work them day and night. Crack the whip! Git 'er done. Motivate people through competition and exploit their intrinsic need for dominance.

It's the ultimate pyramid scheme. You know what a pyramid scheme is, don't you? Pyramid schemes are multi-level organizations that create a system where a few on the top benefit from those at the bottom. Does that sound like a structure that would foster freedom and love? I don't think so either.

But if the pyramid structure is anti-Kingdom, then how should we organize people? There must be leadership in any endeavor. Otherwise, freedom itself becomes chaos and everyone reverts back to self-preservation for survival. *Every man for himself!* And that's a bad idea.

No one is an island. We were created for community. We must work together for both protection and advancement. So there has be structure, and there has be order, right? Right. But "what sort of order?" is the question.

Think of a human body. Our spinal cord brings order and structure to all the parts of our body. It effectively brings life to the body. Yet the body does not exist to serve the spinal cord—the spinal cord exists to serve the body.

Did you get that?

That's exactly what Kingdom leadership is like. The purpose of Kingdom leadership and the supporting structure built up around it is to serve the body. The "body" here means "the collection of people,"—i.e., the congregation, the country, etc.

We can discern whether Kingdom leadership is in play simply by asking one question: "Who's being served?" Is it the leaders? Or the workers? Or the members? Or the constituencies? Or the family members? Who's being served?

Kingdom leaders are supposed to protect and empower people within their spheres, not the other way around. Once again, motive matters. What's in leaders' hearts becomes manifest in how they structure the world around them. When leaders build organizations for self-promotion, it will soon become apparent in the way they govern. If they consolidate all power at the top and recruit people *only* to serve the leader's agenda, then they are leading a pyramid structure organization.

***In the traditional, worldly structure, everything flows up toward the top. But that is not the Kingdom structure that Jesus demonstrated.***

But if they exercise power in order to empower others; if they make room for other leaders to share in decisions and direction; if they get up every morning and lead for the purpose of helping others find their purpose; then *that's* a Kingdom-style organization. In fact, that organization *is* the Kingdom manifest in the world.

The problem with the pyramid structure is that it is upside down. In the traditional, worldly structure, everything flows up toward the top. But that is not the Kingdom structure that Jesus demonstrated. Jesus knelt before His disciples and pushed power up toward them as He washed their feet. The King of all kings served His servants.

In fact, Jesus would not allow His disciples to remain "servants." He made them His friends:

*Greater love has no one than this, that one lay down his life for his friends. You are My friends if you do what I command you.*

*No longer do I call you slaves, for the slave does not know what his master is doing; but I have called you friends, for all things that I have heard from My Father I have made known to you.*

*You did not choose Me but I chose you, and appointed you that you would go and bear fruit, and that your fruit would remain, so that whatever you ask of the Father in My name He may give to you.*

*This I command you, that you love one another. (John 15:13–17)*

Jesus called His disciples "friends" and then laid down His life for them. And He left them only one Kingdom command: "Love one another!"

Jesus did not organize Kingdom leadership structures the way the world does. However, I had overlooked this when I read the New Testament for two reasons:

- First, the way that we humans organize ourselves into pyramids was simply a natural filter for me, simply the way things are. So I didn't even notice that Jesus wasn't following the world's model.
- Second, I *confused headship with hierarchy*, and those are very different things indeed. (We will get deeper into "headship" later on.) Christ's leadership style was actually reversed from our normal model.

It would be easy to think of Kingdom leadership as an inverted triangle—just flip the world's structure on its head. But I think that would actually push the abuse of power to the opposite end with groups of people dominating responsible leaders. Organizations cannot function with power clustered vertically at either end.

No, triangles are simply not a good way to think of the distribution of "power" (love-in-action) in the Kingdom of God. A better way to think of leadership is a circle. In fact, a series of overlapping circles. Think back to "perichoresis," the "circle dance of love" that depicts the inner life of the Trinity. That's how love-manifest-as-power works in the Kingdom. We all move in rhythm with each other as we serve in love. Leaders guide the dance, but everyone contributes to the flow and rhythm.

Another shape that better defines Kingdom authority is the rectangle, and I say that because God revealed His Presence in a rectangular space called "the Temple." When God instructed Moses to build the Tabernacle, and when He explained to David how to build His Temple, He told them both to lay out His sacred space as a rectangular space.

In the New Covenant, God's "rectangular" Temple is built of people:

> *So then you are no longer strangers and aliens, but you are fellow citizens with the saints, and are of God's household, having been built on the foundation of the apostles and prophets, Christ Jesus Himself being the corner stone, in whom the whole building, being fitted together, is growing into a holy temple in the Lord, in whom you also are being built together into a dwelling of God in the Spirit. (Ephesians 2:19–22)*

The Church is God's Temple, and we must be constructed according to God's blueprint. God does not use the same blueprints as the kingdoms of the world. And He absolutely does *not* build His Temple like Babel, a pyramid-ish ziggurat structure that sought to enthrone kings in domination over the earth. I think God's Kingdom blueprint looks more like the Tabernacle of Moses or the Temple of

Solomon than it does the pyramids of Egypt or the ziggurats of Babel.

(*Babel? Babylon? There's that Chaldee spirit again!* See Book 1 for more on the "Chaldee spirit.")

If the Kingdom Jesus is building was a pyramid-based structure with Himself at the very top, then Jesus would be the *cap stone*, the topmost stone placed at the pinnacle of an edifice. And we would all be quite comfortable with that, for that is the power structure with which we are most familiar. After all, Jesus is God. He alone deserves to be at the top! He is the King of kings. He is sovereign. He is worthy of all praise and honor. He is all-powerful—I could go on and on. Yet Jesus did not come to earth to claim the top spot. He came to humble Himself as a servant.

In this Temple, this "dwelling place of God in the Spirit," Jesus is never referred to as the *cap stone*. Rather, He is referred to as the *corner stone*. And there is a huge difference between a cap stone and a corner stone. The cap stone sits at the top; the corner stone sits at the bottom. The corner stone is the first stone laid in the foundation. It is the starting point of the foundation, the first stone laid, and it joins and "squares" the walls. Every stone laid in the building is aligned with the original corner stone.

Psalm 118 says that the stone which builders rejected became the chief corner stone. (Psalm 118:22-23) This verse is so important that all three of the synoptic gospels (Matthew, Mark and Luke) record Jesus quoting this verse. Then Luke brought it up again in the Book of Acts. Paul and Peter also quoted it. Five authors in six New Testament books record that Jesus was the stone rejected by the builders, but God made Him the chief *corner stone*.[3]

This is profoundly important. The emphasis on this verse shows that the idea of a corner stone rather than a cap stone is a strategic clue to building God's Kingdom in your sphere of influence.

The religious system of Jesus' day was pyramid-shaped, which made "cap stone leadership" the only viable power structure. Therefore the religious leaders vehemently rejected Jesus when He came preaching a wildly different form of power, a love-centered power that lays down its life for others. Jesus was an existential threat to everything the entrenched religious bureaucracy had established over generations of religious power. Jesus threatened The Establishment so much that they murdered Him by proxy through the Romans.

> ***Jesus threatened The Establishment so much that they murdered Him.***

And today, humans are still hostile to forms of leadership that originate with love rather than power. We are afraid to love, for love makes us vulnerable. Love requires freedom, and freedom makes people unpredictable. And unpredictability causes volatility, which makes outcomes uncertain. We would much rather establish control-based structures that can guarantee success as we measure it.

Moving away from cap stone leadership to corner stone leadership requires a total paradigm shift. *A pyramid-paradigm shift*. How can you run a business or lead a ministry without being the cap stone? How do we lead people without

---

3 Matthew 21:42, Mark 12:10, Luke 20:17, Acts 4:11, Ephesians 2:20, 1 Peter 2:6-7.

dominating them? Not to sound too simplistic, but we follow Christ's example. He changed the whole world, and He did it without climbing a corporate ladder or manipulating anyone to do His will.

We can, too.

## *Who's the Greatest?*

The shift from *cap stone* to *corner stone* was hard for Jesus' disciples too. Jesus walked closely with these guys for three and a half years, but they still didn't get where His power came from. They thought He was powerful because He stood at the top, like a colossus astride the citadels of power. They believed rightly that Jesus would rule the world as King, but they thought wrongly that His Kingdom would come through an awe-inspiring, overwhelming display of raw power. They wanted Jesus to crush the Romans, cleanse the Temple and restore Israel's dominance over the nations. And they had grand designs on exactly where *they*, as Jesus' top lieutenants, would stand in Jesus' government—at the top, right under the King.

The disciples' fierce ambitions were clearly demonstrated near the end of Jesus' ministry. Jesus had made plans to attend the feast at Jerusalem, but just before leaving the Lord pulled His disciples aside to talk to them about what would happen when He got to the city. He told them that He would be handed over to the Chief Priests and Scribes (religious leaders) who would condemn Him to death. Jesus told them He would then be handed over to Gentiles who would mock, scourge and crucify Him, but on the third day God would raise Him up again.

Remember, Jesus had been teaching about and demonstrating the Kingdom of God for the past three-and-a-half years. The disciples were with Him the whole time. Yet they still envisioned the Kingdom of God in the same form as a worldly kingdom. So, while totally missing the point of Jesus' death in Jerusalem, the disciples instead started vying with each other to see who would get the highest seat of honor, who would wield the greatest power in Messiah's Kingdom.

The Twelve still thought the Kingdom would have a pyramid structure, so they wanted to make sure they were as high up as possible. Remember, in the pyramid structure, value is measured by proximity to power, and all power resides in the top level. Any power exercised lower down is granted from the top.

One of the funniest, and saddest, parts of the story is when James and John enlisted their mother to help them wrangle a promotion out of Jesus. Good ol' mom to the rescue!

> *Then the mother of the sons of Zebedee came to Jesus with her sons, bowing down and making a request of Him. And He said to her, "What do you wish?" She said to Him, "Command that in Your kingdom these two sons of mine may sit one on Your right and one on Your left." (Matthew 20:20-21)*

Thanks, mom!

As I said, that's pretty funny, but also pretty sad. Mom had no idea that her request flowed from a false concept of power. No doubt, as a woman, she lived within a male-dominated, oppressive structure every day, grasping, groping, reaching for any shred of power she could find to improve her lot in life even one smidgen. All she wanted was the best for her boys, and getting them a seat at the head table was her best effort to help. Admirable and sad all at the same time.

The disciples still did not know that Kingdom power and position comes from love and sacrifice rather than from a title or seat at the head table. Kingdom power is demonstrated through love, which is all about the benefit of others. Although Kingdom power certainly blesses its host, it cannot be used for selfish means or the wrong kingdom takes over.

Again, it always comes back to the heart. In God's Kingdom, if you gain access to that kind of power, it will cost you everything, even your life. Love isn't love unless you give it away. Jesus is the perfect example.

Jesus was so gracious in His reply to James and John's dear mother:

> *But Jesus answered, "You do not know what you are asking. Are you able to drink the cup that I am about to drink?" They said to Him, "We are able." He said to them, "My cup you shall drink; but to sit on My right and on My left, this is not Mine to give, but it is for those for whom it has been prepared by My Father."*
>
> *And hearing this, the ten became indignant with the two brothers. (Matthew 20:22-24)*

The other ten disciples got mad because James and John got the jump on them. Bill Johnson jokes that the other ten were probably upset because they didn't bring their mom to Jesus first.

It's interesting that Jesus didn't shame the disciples. He knew that they were simply operating out of all they knew about kingdom structures. But Jesus could not let it pass unaddressed. So, He took the opportunity to teach them a powerful lesson on Kingdom authority. This is Matthew's version of the same lesson recounted in Luke 22.

> *But Jesus called them to Himself and said, "You know that the rulers of the Gentiles lord it over them,*

*and their great men exercise authority over them. It is not this way among you, but whoever wishes to become great among you shall be your servant, and whoever wishes to be first among you shall be your slave; just as the Son of Man did not come to be served, but to serve, and to give His life a ransom for many. (Matthew 20:25-28)*

Jesus makes it explicit: we should only desire positions of leadership within the Kingdom of God because we long to serve people, never because we long for preeminence over people. When we seek positions to gain personal significance —and there is some of this ambition in all of us!—we import a foreign kingdom structure into the Kingdom of God. And when we do that, we get the weakened alloy of leadership that we saw above, a Kingdom that cannot influence the world because it is beholden to it.

***We should only desire positions of leadership within the Kingdom of God because we long to serve people, never because we long for preeminence over people.***

If you desire to lead in the Kingdom because you're trying to climb the people-power-pyramid, then you desire to serve for the wrong reasons. And it doesn't mean that you are neither called nor qualified. God may be truly drawing you to lead in His Kingdom. But Holy Spirit is calling us all to surrender the brokenness that causes us to seek positions of power for validation from others. If significance and success is what's driving us rather than serving in love, then we need Holy Spirit to heal our broken, fearful heart.

And that's exactly what He will do!

Let's be clear. I am not saying that the desire to achieve significance and success is wrong. Not at all. All I'm saying is that we must be alert to *how* we seek to achieve these things. God created us for greatness and glory, but the only path to greatness and glory in God's Kingdom is through love.

We must voluntarily serve those around us. We must lift them up and help them become all they can be. When we all do this, the tide rises and everyone on the ship goes higher. It's a corporate thing. We are more connected than we have been taught, and we are more dependent on each other than we want to believe.

Jesus did not rebuke His disciples for wanting greatness. The desire for greatness and glory is hardwired into us by our Creator. Rather, Jesus showed them how to achieve it properly. Great people serve others first. To be "first," to be the best, we must serve others with such intensity that we purposefully slave away for them.

When the disciples reminded Jesus that they gave up everything for Him, He talked to them about ruling and reigning, about great rewards, and then He proclaimed the heart of the gospel message: "But many who are first will be last; and the last, first." (Matthew 19:30; 20:16; Mark 9:35; 10:31; Luke 13:30)

The way up is down!

Jesus illustrated His point with a powerful visual:

> *At that time the disciples came to Jesus and said, "Who then is greatest in the kingdom of heaven?" And He called a child to Himself and set him before them, and said, "Truly I say to you, unless you are converted and become like children, you will not enter the kingdom of heaven. Whoever then humbles himself as this child, he is the greatest in the kingdom of heaven." (Matthew 18:1-4)*

Jesus is the King of kings, yet He walked in complete humility. (1Timothy 6:15) He was the most powerful person in their group. In fact, He was the most powerful person on the planet! He had power to heal people. He paid taxes with money drawn from the mouth of a fish. He fed thousands with a little boy's lunch. Shoot, Jesus even raised the dead! Now, that's true power. If anyone could have claimed a top spot on the pyramid, Jesus could have. Yet Jesus "did not come to be served but to serve, and to give His life as a ransom for many" (Matthew 20:28).

Jesus came to serve and establish our connection with God's heart. He came to establish the Kingdom of Heaven on earth, and He demonstrated in glorious splendor just how it is done. Jesus did not start giving His life away at the cross, although that was His ultimate sacrifice. No, Jesus gave His life away every day by serving those around Him, by loving and by living from a supernatural Kingdom. He loved and empowered those connected to Him. And, right now, King Jesus is still encouraging and empowering us to do even greater things. (John 14:12)

Even though Jesus was the most powerful human on the planet, He refused to scale the heights of the power-pyramid so that He could rule arbitrarily over us. Satan gave Jesus the chance to buy into that false kingdom when he tempted Christ in the wilderness. But Jesus refused. That would build the wrong kingdom. Instead, the One who was greatest went low to lift us up. He refused to build a world-wide empire to feed His ego or to gain power. He was already omnipotent, and He had nothing to prove except His love for you and me. Now, He wants us to do the same for the world around us.

One last thing. The great pyramids of Egypt are glorified tombs. They house the decaying corpses and relics of glories long past. They preserve for generations to see what happens to the kingdoms of the world. And that's exactly what happens to the Church when we embrace the dead systems of human supremacy. All humans revert to the same level when they are lowered in the ground. There is no supremacy in the graveyard.

We have a choice to make: humble ourselves now and be exalted with Christ forever, or pursue proud power over people now and be leveled at the end. As for me, I reject the ancient pyramid scheme for the grand experiment of world transforming love.

# CHAPTER 7

# ROYAL IDENTITY

The clash of kingdoms starts in the heart. In fact, the original power-pyramid was an inverted heart, a human heart turned upside down due to sin. Before Christ came to save us, our heart was "more deceitful than all else" and "desperately sick" (Jeremiah 17:9–10). As Jesus said,

> *For out of the heart come evil thoughts, murders, adulteries, fornications, thefts, false witness, slanders. (Matthew 15:19)*

Thankfully, in Christ, our heart is transformed, and we no longer live under the curse of sin and death. But the fallen heart is a battlefield. The heart became the channel for evil when it was detached from the life of God through deception and disobedience. Just like fleshly bodies deteriorate when life ebbs away, so our heart decays when it is alienated from the life of God. As Paul said,

> *So this I say, and affirm together with the Lord, that you walk no longer just as the Gentiles also walk, in the futility of their mind, being darkened in their understanding, excluded ("alienated" — ESV) from the life of God because of the ignorance that is in them, because of the hardness of their heart; and they, having become callous, have given themselves over to sensuality for the practice of every kind of impurity with greediness. (Ephesians 4:17–19)*

The human heart was created in the image and likeness of God. When humans sinned, they shattered the image of

God manifest within them by turning away from the Father and seeking identity through supremacy over each other. Their eyes were "opened," and they beheld each other's nakedness, their weakness, their lack. Their guilt and shame provoked rivalry as they pointed fingers at each other and at the serpent, trying to find someone—anyone!—to take the blame for what they'd done. Their perfect unity was fragmented in an instant into competition and conflict.

That's the genesis of the wrong kingdom.

I want you to see that the clash of kingdoms started in the division between Adam and Eve. I want you to see that it started *in the human heart*. When their heart was darkened though sin toward God and toward one another, an evil kingdom rooted in hostility broke out into the world.

***The clash of kingdoms started in the division between Adam and Eve.***

This hostile kingdom metastasized throughout the nations as satan's kingdom. Indeed, it was Jesus Himself who identified the global domain of darkness that emanates from the fallen heart as satan's kingdom. (Matthew 12:26) When Jesus came, He broke the tyranny of the dark kingdom by exposing the lie that gave it power. Jesus defeated the dark kingdom by delivering the human heart. As Paul said, Jesus "rescued us from the domain of darkness, and transferred us to the kingdom of His beloved Son" (Colossians 1:13). Paul also recounted how Jesus told him:

> *To open their eyes so that they may turn from darkness to light and from the dominion of Satan to God, that they may receive forgiveness of sins and an inheritance among those who have been sanctified by faith in Me. (Acts 26:18)*

The "forgiveness of sins" resolved the heart issue. And embedded within this forgiveness was a restoration to "an inheritance among those who have been sanctified by faith in Me." The inheritance is the earth itself, as Psalm 2 makes clear, and the restoration of inheritance entails the restoration of identity. By being restored as children of God, we are made "fellow heirs" with the Son of God. (Romans 8:16-17)

Because the clash of kingdoms started in the human heart, it became an identity crisis. Adam and Eve lost sight of who they were as the image of God when they sought godlikeness apart from communion with their Creator. Their identity was no longer rooted in who they were before God, but now, in their darkened, fearful mind, their identity was rooted in who they were in comparison to others.

Fear caused them to believe God was holding out on them, and that the other person—that one over there hiding in the bushes!—was competing with them for supremacy. The lie took root in their mind and became pride and insecurity.

I remember once when about to teach a course on the women's issue, I knew I had to deal with an edgy defensiveness I often felt when sharing about this issue. I felt the pressure to prove my point, to defend my arguments. I would even feel a little combative. This was not the first time I felt this way, but I knew it had to be the last. However, I didn't know where that edginess was coming from or how to turn it off. I had tried. I had prayed. But it was still there.

So I asked a lady from church to meet with me for an inner healing session where I could process what was happening in my heart. While processing with her, in my mind I saw a coin in my hand. On one side was the word "pride" and on the other side was the word "insecurity." They were two sides of the same coin—and this was *my* coin. It was my pride and my insecurity.

Jesus was there, and He wanted to give me a different coin. He wanted to make an exchange with me, but I just couldn't. Then Holy Spirit took me back to a scene in my childhood where I felt pressured to defend my assertion that I hadn't stolen change from my father. (Actually, I had!) In that moment, I relived the shame and anger from my childhood. Holy Spirit revealed to me that the fear of being wrong, of being exposed as dishonest, of being rejected, had made me unnecessarily defensive when preparing to present a controversial topic. Thankfully, as I repented for lying and stealing as a child, He healed me in that encounter.

Then—and here's the big breakthrough!—He told me that truth didn't have to be defended, it just needed to be shared. I was able to make an exchange with Jesus and receive the coin He wanted me to have instead. On one side it said "love" and on the other side was "confidence." I traded in pride and insecurity for love and confidence. What an exchange!

That battle I faced with pride and insecurity is much like what happened to the first humans when they sinned. Through fear, they withdrew from fellowship with the Father and one another. The beauty of perichoretic love was marred by suspicion. They lost sight of who they were.

When identity gets tangled up with pride and insecurity, it produces a need for supremacy. However, when we see who we are in relation to our Creator, which is the heart of true humility—seeing ourselves as God sees us—we no longer need to compete with others. When the Kingdom comes through the indwelling power of the Holy Spirit, He transforms the deep-seated center of human identity so that who we are flows from our relationship to the Father rather than from others' perception and acceptance of who we are. Then, in Christ, we no longer need to scale the pyramid. The heart is set right side up.

The first humans were created to be sons and daughters of the King. Which meant, by definition, that they were destined to become kings as well. Kingship is inherited. Of course, some kings gain their crown through insurrection, but legitimate kings receive the right to rule from their father and mother before them. That's exactly what made Adam and Eve kings—they were children of the Great King.

Before sin, Adam and Eve derived their royal identity from their relation to God, not from their competition with one another. They did not ascend to their thrones of creational dominion by climbing, clambering and stomping on each other. Their position was not achieved in relation to each other, but in relation to God: they were kings because they were sons.

After sin distorted their identity through the lie that turned their heart away from God as their source, humans then pursued power over each other. Now, to their deluded minds, the only way to achieve godlikeness was to prevail over others. Godlikeness through supremacy. Rather than partnering with each other in the royal identity that was freely given by grace, men and women declared war on each other in a futile, fruitless quest for significance through domination.

It was the beginning of the gender wars.

When the Kingdom of God breaks through in our heart, Holy Spirit immediately sets out to restore our identity as sons and daughters of the King. The lie of significance through competition is exposed and the truth of who we are in Christ is restored. We are recreated in the image of God and seated with King Jesus in His Father's throne. As Holy

Spirit releases who we were originally designed to be as the image of God, we start walking into the kingly identity we were created to carry.

The Kingdom of God coming to fruition in the world depends on people discovering their royal identity. As we discover who we are, we release who we are into the world. Which means, if we want to see the Kingdom unleashed in the world, we must first see the Kingdom unleashed in you and me. We must see the Kingdom unleashed in our heart.

## *Positional Truth vs. Conditional Truth*

Knowing who we are manifests Kingdom reality. But sometimes knowing who we are means believing what God says about who we are even when we are not currently manifesting who He says we are. God calls us sons, but sometimes we behave like orphans. Why? Because we have trouble believing what God says. Which is how the whole sin thing started.

Some people call the difference between what God says about us and how we actually live every day the difference between *positional truth* and *conditional truth*. For example, a positional truth is I have "become the righteousness of Christ" (2 Corinthians 5:21). His righteousness has been allocated to my account freely by grace. I don't have to do anything to earn it. The state of righteousness is a position that I occupy simply by virtue of being born again.

However, sometimes I do not live up to the reality of who I am. This is the other side of righteousness, the conditional side. This is the conditional reality into which I am growing. And the amazing thing is, the conditional shifts as I become aware of the positional. In other words, when I believe that I am righteous in Christ through no effort of my own, the Spirit of Christ within me produces the righteousness that is mine. I manifest whatever I am aware of.

We sometimes struggle with embracing a regality-reality that doesn't seem real. To profess royal identity when we behave like paupers sometimes seems disingenuous. In fact, when I first heard someone teaching that we *are* righteous even when we don't behave righteously, I resisted fiercely. I was just certain that we were being fed total heresy.

There I sat, perched sanctimoniously on my little chair, just fuming at the preacher. How dare he? How dare he say that we are no longer sinners? Because I knew good and well that I was a sinner. Sure, I was saved, born again, but I had been trained to believe that I was still stuck in my sins until the resurrection. I had been trained to believe that sin still had the rule over me. I certainly had never heard that I had the rule over sin. Boy, was I mad!

***We empower the wrong kingdom when we believe a lie.***

When I went home, I began to process with the Lord. "Father God, show me if there's any truth to that, because I am really upset." And He answered me. He began to show me who I was in Christ. The King of kings started showing me my royal identity. That preacher was right, darn it. I just didn't have that revelation yet. And God had to show me that. No person could show me. The only way to really know who you are as a king in the Kingdom is to be reoriented by supernatural revelation back to who you were first created to be.

And then you must walk it out. You must bring the conditional into alignment with the positional through the power of Holy Spirit infused faith. We empower the wrong kingdom when we believe a lie. We unleash the right

Kingdom when we believe the truth, when we believe that we are kings right here, right now, even when it doesn't appear true.

The most amazing thing about faith is that it believes what God says is true even when it does not yet appear to be true. And by the simple act of believing, faith makes it true. Faith *realizes* and *manifests* what is true. Faith makes the true *real*. Faith looks past what I see around me and perceives what I see above me, the reality of heaven, and by seeing it manifests it. Faith envisions the Word, and Word becomes flesh.

My position as a king reigning in life with Him is based on faith. It is based on what He did at the cross. I am a king simply because my Father is the King of kings. My kingship is based on what He did. He made me a king because He loves me and He adopted me into his family. I am now a king based on my rebirth. Not based on anything that I deserve at all. It's totally based on His love for me.

Satan convinced humans to disobey the voice of God simply by making them look away from what they *already had* to what they could (theoretically) gain with human effort. He promised them a godlikeness that they already had. *They were already like God.* They possessed positional regency, but satan made them doubt it. He shifted their focus away from who they were to whom they supposed they were not. Satan taught them to surmise that ruling as gods was outside their reach. If only they could eat of the tree, then—then and only then!—they could be wise, knowing good and evil.

It was a lie.

And it is still a lie today. When satan tells you that you are not kingly, that you are just not royal material, he is lying. You are already a king and a priest with Christ. Believe it!

Satan tried the same tactic on Jesus: "If you are the Son of God…" *If* you are. What a joke! Jesus had just heard the Father declare, "This is My Son, in Whom I am well pleased." Jesus refused to entertain the voice of the enemy for even one moment. He had nothing to prove. He chose to live in the proceeding word of God and declared, "It is written…" Jesus chose to live in the positional reality that He possessed due to the simple fact of who He was.

Can you believe that God calls you a king and walk it out? Will you begin to operate and start influencing the world around you as if you are a king? As if you already have that kind of influence, that kind of power and that kind of authority? Because *you already do!* Believe me, Satan is after your identity. If he can get that, the rest doesn't matter. If you agree with his lies, you will empower his kingdom by agreeing that you are insignificant.

Stop believing lies.

### *Pauper Mentality*

The awareness through faith of our God-derived royal identity breaks the *pauper mentality.* The pauper mentality believes wrongly that success and significance are a zero sum game, and glory can only be achieved by taking it away from others. When the first humans believed the lie that godlikeness is an objective *thing* that can be obtained outside of relationship with God, a piece of fruit to be seized and consumed, then the fight was on. Gotta grab my "apple" before you get yours. Since there's only a finite number of apples available, and apples are the source of my significance, I'd better make sure I get mine before you do. In fact, I'd better steal yours to make sure you don't get more apples than me.

Substitute wealth, power, position, prestige, possessions, success, significance—on and on—in the place of "apples" and you get the point: when our significance comes from things outside of God, then we must compete for those things. That is the *pauper mentality,* the *poverty mindset.* There's never enough, so I'd better hoard what I can, beg, steal or borrow, whatever it takes to ensure my survival.

But when my royal identity comes from God, the supply of glory is inexhaustible. My success is no longer measured against your success. We are not fighting over apples. I am a king because my Father is the King, not because I triumphed over you in the struggle for more apples. Apples are limitless when I receive them from the hand of my Father. I can share apples with you, give them freely away, imitating the kindness of my Father, because I do not fear the lack of apples. If I need more apples, they are readily available from my Father's hand. So why should I fuss with you over apples?

> ***Religion promotes a false humility rooted in the pauper mentality.***

Since my Father created apples by the power of His Word, I should never fear that He will run out of apples. He can simply speak His Word over my life, and apples grow by the bushels. Again, fill in the "apples" blank with whatever we need for success in life: wealth, power, position, whatever. When these things come from the hand of God, there's always enough. Fear of lack is broken, and the need to fight for prominence is ended. If I run out of apples, I turn to Him, not against you.

We were created for glory. "It is your Father's good pleasure to give you the Kingdom" (Luke 12:32 ESV). And the royal identity we were given in Christ never robs another of their royal identity. Glory is not a zero sum game, like finite pieces of the pie—apple pie, of course!—over which we must compete. Glory flows from the infinite nature of God, and when I'm blessed, or you're blessed, the blessing of one does not diminish the blessing of another.

Another aspect of the pauper mentality is that God doesn't have enough glory to share. Religion teaches us that we must not pursue glory, for that would require stealing it from God, who alone is worthy of glory. Religion promotes a false humility rooted in the pauper mentality, in the idea that there is never enough. For religion, glory is indeed a zero sum game: if you and I are glorified, then God's glory is diminished.

But this is flat wrong. God created us for glory. He crowned us as kings. And our kingship does not diminish his supreme Kingship. Remember, the Supreme Being could be the ultimate supremacist, but He is not. Why? Because He does not fear the loss of His glory. Supremacy is rooted in fear. God shares kingship because His Kingship is not threatened. He knows who He is!

We are often warned against "taking God's glory." We read, "My glory I will not give to another," (Isaiah 48:11) and think that our role before God must be humiliation and subjugation. But this is a total misunderstanding. The scripture quoted here is a reference to false gods, to idols. God will not give His glory to another god. He also will not permit proud humans to claim the glory apart from Him:

> *That no flesh should glory in His presence. (1 Corinthians 1:29 KJV)*

But both of these warnings are to those who seek glory outside of Him, a false glory that is actually the pride that promotes rivalry. God will not *give* His glory, but He does *share* it. To be saved is to have "Christ in you, the hope of glory" (Colossians 1:27). To be saved is to be "glorified" (Romans 8:30). We were created to be "crowned...with glory and honor...[and] given...dominion over the works of [His] hands" (Psalm 8:5–6 ESV). To see God's glory as a finite commodity that we must never steal is to reduce His glory down to another apple that we must not eat. That's just another way that religion robs us of our original destiny. It's false humility. It's a pauper mentality.

It is not glorifying God to diminish your self. God created you to be a king and to rule with Him. He did not fear that your coronation as king would take anything away from His rule. And Jesus also knew that. He showed us how it's done. He did not grasp desperately for equality with God. (Philippians 2:6) Jesus possessed equality with God simply by virtue of His relation to the Father, through His Sonship. Therefore, He could willingly lay aside His divine prerogatives without fear of loss—the original "prince and the pauper" story. He was never worried about who He was. He just announced confidently, "I'm the Son of God." And so are we.

If we have a pauper mentality, we're always going to be looking at our lack, at what we do not have in comparison to what others have. Females are less than males. The poor are less than the rich. Minorities are less than the majority. The old are less than the young. The masses are less than the elites. All of this is rooted in false comparisons. But when we discover our royal identity, then our focus is on who we are in Christ. Our significance is no longer measured in comparison to others.

The pauper mentality is full of excuses, finger-pointing and blame-gaming. But royal identity receives authority and accepts responsibility. Royal identity lives only to hear, "Well done, my good and faithful servant!" Royal identity thrives on, "This is my beloved son in whom I am well pleased!" Royal identity receives correction without shame, for divine correction calls us to measure up to who we were created to be in Christ. The Father's correction points us to who we are, not to who we are *not*.

I once studied through a series taught by Kris Vallotton called *From Paupers to Princes*.[1] Kris taught from Proverbs,

> *There are three things that make the earth tremble. No four it cannot endure. The earth can't endure a pauper who becomes a king. (Proverbs 30:21-22)*

The earth shakes. That reminds me of Romans 8 where creation stands on tiptoe, crying out, straining to see the sons of God as they manifest. (Romans 8:19) The earth trembles when a pauper becomes a king. Why? Because the planet dreads a pauper's tyranny. A pauper rules harshly, fearfully, paranoid about enemies and schemers. Because a pauper's rule is rooted in his or her supremacy over others, brutal imposition of power is the only strategy for leading.

A pauper has no true sense of identity. Their significance is derived from their dominance over others. A pauper lives in fear of never having enough. So, they are always grasping, getting, taking, stealing. They don't know that all the apples they will ever need are in the hand of their heavenly Father. So they desperately seize all the apples they can from everyone around them.

Noble kings serve for the good of their citizens. A noble king rides through his realm seeing what he can do for the people. A pauper king rides through the kingdom seeing what he can take, what he can get. No wonder the earth trembles when a pauper becomes a king.

---

[1] Available at kvministries.org.

A pauper feels like no one really values or cares about them. It's every man for himself. Dog-eat-dog. Eat or get eaten. Win or die. Say and do whatever it takes to dominate others. Get ahead at all costs. But this fearful mindset is broken in Christ. When you know who you are in Christ, then you climb out of the boxing ring and withdraw from the fight. No need to fight for something I already have freely in Christ.

Another reason the earth cringes when paupers rule is that paupers never know the power of their words. Fear drives paupers to use their words as weapons. And when paupers gain authority over people, their words become decrees that shape reality—a dark, dreadful reality. When paupers lead, whether in families, business, churches or nations, toxic cultures grow up around them. Hostility becomes the underlying spirit that drives everyone under a pauper's rule. Everyone is on defense, trying just to survive. Ever lived, worked or served in an environment like that?

A pauper believes deep down that they are insignificant. They feel naked and ashamed. They spend their life pointing fingers at everyone else. It's everyone else's fault that they are failing. And they *always* feel like they're failing, no matter how successful they may appear. This is what drives workaholism and perfectionism. There's just never enough.

Let me declare it over you right now: *You are significant.* You are not a pauper. You are positioned as a king, seated in the heavens with Christ on His Father's throne. That's true about you whether or not you believe it. If the enemy has been telling you that you are a nobody, let me expose his lie: *you are somebody because your Daddy is the King of all creation!* You are somebody because the ultimate Somebody created you in His image. I'm not sure where you learned that you are not enough. Maybe your family? Maybe in second grade when you were terrified to bring home a report card with anything less than straight A's? But wherever you learned it, in the mighty name of Jesus, I declare that the lie is broken!

I declare in Jesus' name that your true identity in Christ is being released *right now!* Your "true self," the self you were created to be in Christ, is rising to the surface. You are already who you are in Jesus, but you must rise to the occasion—the occasion of discovering who you were created to be! You are beloved. You are accepted. There is nothing you can do to get accepted or unaccepted—your acceptance was gained for you by Christ, through His perfect obedience to the Father. The true you is hidden in Him, already bought and paid for.

***There is nothing you can do to get accepted or unaccepted—your acceptance was gained for you by Christ, through His perfect obedience to the Father.***

I release over you right now the astonishing truth that God adores you. No matter what you've done. He adores you because you are His. Period. He is not ashamed of what you've done. Sin doesn't surprise Him, and neither does it make Him turn away from you. The idea that God turns His face away from you when you sin is a myth, a distortion of what happened at the cross. God never turned away from Jesus, and He doesn't turn away from you. You may feel like He does, but that lie is only true in your mind. Stop believing it!

God is not ashamed of who you are. Paul said that God loved us while we were sinners. He didn't wait until we cleaned up our act to love us. No, His love is what cleans up our act! No wonder the enemy wants to sabotage your acceptance of the Father's love. It is His love that transforms us into who we already are in Him. Every part of your brain that believes the lie that you must earn the Father's love is being healed right now. Every lie is broken *now,* in Jesus' name. It is done now. Receive it.

## *The Spirit of Poverty*

The pauper mentality is how we think. But how we think can become something much more sinister as our thinking comes into alignment with the prevailing spirit of the age, what Paul calls "the course of the world" (Ephesians 2:2). Sort of like mental WiFi that logs on to a global network. Our pauper mentality can become stinking-thinking on steroids. Mob mentality, group-think, call it what you will. But when the pauper mentality gets tangled up with demonic influences that seek to dominate the human race, it becomes *a spirit of poverty*. And a spirit of poverty controls much more than just money. It is an overall mindset of how you view all of life.

And a spirit of poverty is more than just a human mindset. It is an ingrained mindset exploited strategically by evil spirits to enslave humans for generations in patterns and cycles of poverty that seek to prevent the blessing of Abraham from taking hold in every nation under heaven.

The story of Moses leading Israel out of Egypt is one of the best examples of how a pauper mentality can take hold on a national and generational level. In fact, the Israel story is the Adam and Eve story writ large, the story of what the Fall looks like on a national scale. Just as Adam failed in the garden to live out his call to dominion over the earth, so Israel failed in the Promised Land to live out the blessing of Abraham. And it all comes down to an ingrained spirit of poverty.

The contrast between Moses and Israel demonstrates the difference between a pauper mentality and royal identity. Moses was raised in Pharaoh's house to be a king. As Stephen tells us in Acts 7, Moses knew he was meant to be Israel's deliverer. He carried that innate sense of destiny within him. Yet when Moses went out at forty years old to see his people, they could not see what Moses saw. They were blinded by their circumstances. Moses saw past the circumstances because he was trained to see the possible, not the actual. That's what kings do: they envision the possible.

Regardless, the Hebrews couldn't see beyond their shackles, and, after killing an Egyptian overseer for abusing a Hebrew slave, Moses fled the nation, devastated by Israel's rejection. He was shocked that they didn't understand who he was. Forty years later, after spending a third of his life keeping sheep on the backside of the desert, Moses returns to Egypt under a powerful, kingly mandate to lead out Yahweh's people.

Israel still did not believe.

Finally, after a series of dramatic miracles, Moses gets the people out of Egypt, and they camp at the foot of Mt. Sinai where God attempts to shape them into a new nation. The Lord God announces with great delight that Israel is called to be "a kingdom of priests and a holy nation" (Exodus 19:6), which literally means a holy nation of "kings and priests." God's intention for His people was always that worship and dominion would go together.

It didn't go well. Why? Because Israel had a pauper mentality—actually, a *slave mentality*—and could not see themselves as the kings and priests they were called to be. And, repeatedly, the pauper mentality exploded into a mob mentality where the entire nation rose up in defiant unbelief. The pauper mentality actually became a prevailing *spirit of poverty* that defined an entire generation. They rebelled ten times, as the Lord put it, and He turned them over to the fate they wished upon themselves:

> *Then all the congregation lifted up their voices and cried, and the people wept that night. All the sons of Israel grumbled against Moses and Aaron; and the whole congregation said to them, "Would that we had died in the land of Egypt! Or would that we had died in this wilderness! Why is the Lord bringing us into this land, to fall by the sword? Our wives and our little ones will become plunder; would it not be better for us to return to Egypt?" So they said to one another, "Let us appoint a leader and return to Egypt." (Numbers 14:1–4)*

The problem was that Moses got the slaves out of Egypt, but God couldn't get the slavery out of them. An entire generation died in the wilderness. Of all the men over twenty years of age who were qualified for the army, only Joshua and Caleb made it into the Land of Promise.

> ***The problem was that Moses got the slaves out of Egypt, but God couldn't get the slavery out of them.***

Why didn't the other million plus people make it into the Promised Land? They didn't believe they could. And they didn't just refuse to believe as individuals—the entire congregation succumbed to a prevailing spirit that defined the culture of more than a million people. You have to wonder how many individuals would have joined Joshua and Caleb in reckless faith if they had not been caught up in the spirit of poverty that carried the nation along like a raging torrent.

Israel was sucked into a vortex of unbelief all because they measured themselves by their conditional reality rather than their positional reality. They refused to see themselves as God saw them. Here's how God saw them:

> *For you are a holy people to the Lord your God; the Lord your God has chosen you to be a people for His own possession out of all the peoples who are on the face of the earth. The Lord did not set His love on you nor choose you because you were more in number than any of the peoples, for you were the fewest of all peoples, but because the Lord loved you and kept the oath which He swore to your forefathers, the Lord brought you out by a mighty hand and redeemed you from the house of slavery, from the hand of Pharaoh king of Egypt. (Deuteronomy 7:6–8)*

But here's how Israel saw themselves,

> *But the men who had gone up with him said, "We are not able to go up against the people, for they are too strong for us." So they gave out to the sons of Israel a bad report of the land which they had spied out, saying, "The land through which we have gone, in spying it out, is a land that devours its inhabitants; and all the people whom we saw in it are men of great size. There also we saw the Nephilim (the sons of Anak are part of the Nephilim); and we became like grasshoppers in our own sight, and so we were in their sight." (Numbers 13:31–33)*

Israel sabotaged their own destiny by partnering with a lying spirit that whispered how unprepared and unable they were to take the land. Israel's pauper mentality had become a spirit of poverty that possessed the hearts and minds of more than a million people. Rather than see themselves as God saw them—and rather than turning their hearts in faith toward the mighty power of God!—they focused on how they saw themselves in comparison to the giants: "We became like grasshoppers in our own sight, and so we were in their sight."

How the Hebrews saw themselves manifested. Their thoughts and words became actions. A false self-evaluation became their actual reality.

How you see yourself matters. Do you see yourself as a king? Do you embrace your royal identity? There is something about a pervasive spirit of poverty that seems to constantly drag people back down into the abyss. So often we see people reap windfall incomes, maybe they win the lottery or receive a huge inheritance, and in just a few months or years, they are broke again. While the opposite happens with many wealthy people: they lose it all and recover everything over and over. I've heard that most millionaires have been totally broke, even bankrupt, more than once.

Why do wealthy people rebound so often? Simply this: *they do not see themselves as poor*. A lack of money doesn't define them. They see prosperity as inherent to who they are. They have a wealthy mindset.

Why do the poor often end up back in poverty even after gaining great wealth? *They see themselves as poor*. So, no matter how much money they get, they still subconsciously see themselves as broke. So, quite soon, they are.

It's all about identity. Do you see yourself as God sees you? Think about Joseph: unwillingly sold into slavery, yet the slavery never got in him. What about Daniel? He was born a noble in Israel, then taken away into captivity, most likely castrated and made a eunuch of the Babylonian king. But he never lost his royal identity. David was a shepherd, but he possessed the heart of a king. On and on, countless examples abound of people in the Bible and throughout history who never allowed their surroundings or their circumstances to determine their internal reality. They saw themselves as kings, so that's what they became.

## *Women and Royal Identity*

Let me say it again: the clash of kingdoms started as an *identity* crisis. Adam and Eve lost sight of who they were as the image of God when they sought godlikeness apart from communion with their Creator. Their identity was no longer rooted in who they were before God, but now, in their darkened and fearful mind, it was rooted in who they were in comparison to others—specifically, in comparison to the opposite gender.

Men and women were reduced to identifying themselves in contrast to and in competition with each other. Men sought significance through supremacy, and women sought control through manipulation. Both retreated into base reactions to the other, and both lost their sense of who they were in relation to God. The gospel fixed that. The royal identity of both men and women was restored in the resurrection of Jesus when the curse was broken and the new creation was revealed.

Our restored identity in Christ is the basis for restored unity. Because the new birth reorients our sense of who we are back to our relation to God rather than in competition with each other, we can now get along like never before. Conflict dissolves into love, and hostility into humility. I don't need to be superior to you or anyone. I can serve you in genuine humility because I know who I am. As Paul said, we are called to walk "with all humility and gentleness, with patience, showing tolerance for one another in love, being diligent to preserve the unity of the Spirit in the bond of peace" (Ephesians 4:2–3).

In Colossians 3, Paul explicitly connects identity with unity:

> *Do not lie to one another, since you laid aside the old self with its evil practices, and have put on the new self who is being renewed to a true knowledge according to the image of the One who created him—a renewal in which there is no distinction between Greek and Jew, circumcised and uncircumcised, barbarian, Scythian, slave and freeman, but Christ is all, and in all.*

Let me interrupt. Did you see that? We refuse to lie to each other because we have "put on the new self." The new self is "renewed to a true knowledge" and recreated "according to the image of the One." This renewal erases all human divisions, for "Christ is all, and in all." Do you see that? Unity flows from our new identity.

Now, back to Paul's powerful word:

> *So, as those who have been chosen of God, holy and beloved, put on a heart of compassion, kindness, humility, gentleness and patience; bearing with one another, and forgiving each other, whoever has a complaint against anyone; just as the Lord forgave you, so also should you.*
>
> *Beyond all these things put on love, which is the perfect bond of unity. Let the peace of Christ rule in your hearts, to which indeed you were called in one body; and be thankful. (Colossians 3:9–15)*

Above all else, Paul exhorts, "put on love, which is the perfect bond of unity." And that will produce peace.

As I said in Chapter 1, the move of God that's happening is a *unity through identity* movement that totally reorganizes the structures of human society. By bringing people into the true *identity* for which they were created, the royal identity hidden for them in Christ before the foundation of the world, Holy Spirit is forging a new human *unity* rooted in the reconciliation purchased for us by Christ at the cross. Our reconciliation with God produces reconciliation with one another.

Peter specifically connects our sense of royal identity with how we behave toward others:

> *But you are a chosen race, a royal priesthood, a holy nation, a people for God's own possession, so that you may proclaim the excellencies of Him who has called you out of darkness into His marvelous light. (1 Peter 2:9)*

Understanding the *excellency* of your identity and heritage in Christ totally transforms how you live in the world. A sense of who you are brings a sense of how you should then live. Royal identity brings real unity.

Getting a revelation of our royal identity unleashes the Kingdom in a profoundly real-world way. This is particularly true with regard to gender issues. Our royal identity is rooted in who we are in Christ, and in Christ there is no longer "male and female." This doesn't mean, of course, that biological gender is erased, but it does mean that gender distinctions arising from the Fall and enshrined in human culture *are* erased. (Galatians 3:28)

**_Getting a revelation of our royal identity unleashes the Kingdom in a profoundly real-world way._**

Did you know women can be kings? Women can be leaders. In fact, the New Testament is filled with examples of women leading in ways that first century culture—and much of twenty-first century culture!—did not approve.

For example, Paul referred to Phoebe as a deacon and leader in the church at Cenchrea. (Romans 16:1-2) Translators were uncomfortable rendering exactly as it reads, so they rendered "deacon" (*diakonos*) as "servant" and reduced the word "leader" (*prostatis*) down to "helper." That's too bad. The truth has been obscured, but Phoebe was a full-fledged deacon of the church at Cenchrea and a leader —even a *ruler*—to many including Paul. Actually, the Contemporary English Version does a great job of translating that verse as "she was a respected leader of many others, including myself."

Also, Phoebe was entrusted with Paul's letter to the Romans, and most likely was the first one to read it to the churches at Rome. Isn't it amazing that the first time *Romans* was preached, it was a woman doing the preaching! Such divine irony.

Another powerful woman whom Paul mentioned in Romans 16 as leading the New Testament Church was Junia:

> *Greet Andronicus and Junia, my kinsmen and my fellow prisoners, who are outstanding among the apostles, who also were in Christ before me. (Romans 16:7)*

Junia was most likely married to Andronicus. She was Paul's relative. She was in prison for the gospel and had converted to the Christian faith before Paul. But the most notable thing about Junia is that she was an apostle, and she was "outstanding" among them. Translators didn't like this either. By the 1200s, a copyist had changed the spelling from the feminine "Junia" to the masculine "Junias." Fixed that!

Isn't it sad that men changed the Bible in order to scrub out the fact that women were *apostles* in the New Testament? Pretty unbelievable. But it just shows how pervasive misogyny has been throughout the ages even within the Church.

Then there's the most famous of all women leaders in the New Testament, Priscilla. She's also called Prisca. She's mentioned six times in the New Testament. Most of those times she is mentioned before her husband, which would have been an egregious breach of protocol in the first century. But Jesus and Paul broke protocol quite deliberately, doing everything in their power to loosen the stranglehold that men had on the world.

Priscilla and Aquila were a powerhouse team, co-pastors of a church in their house. They both traveled extensively with Paul. They both taught Apollos "more accurately" in the way of Jesus—again, a terrible breach of protocol if the gospel hadn't radically liberated women.

What about other notable women? Philip's four daughters prophesied. Ten women are mentioned by name in Romans 16, seven of whom are lauded for their public ministry, Phoebe and Junia among them. Chloe is mentioned in 1 Corinthians 1. And many others.

The Holy Spirit was poured out on both men and women, making prophecy available to both. The gifts of the Spirit were divided severally to all who receive the Spirit, which includes women. Over and over the New Testament demonstrates that women are not defined by their gender but by their call. Women, just like men, are called and gifted by the Lord Jesus Christ to lead with power. All this shows that royal identity was restored to both men and women in the new creation.

And as we walk into our royal identity, the Kingdom walks into the world with us. Men and women no longer feel the need to compete. Male supremacy starts looking ridiculous. Why would any man need to suppress the "weaker sex" to demonstrate strength? Obviously, he doesn't. Neither does he need to patronize women with a false chivalry that masks contempt. Men who walk in royal identity have only one goal: to serve others in love. Supremacy is not ever an option.

Do you see how understanding the Kingdom and the royal identity we have before our King utterly transforms the way we serve each other? My five-year Kingdom journey now starts to make sense. And there's more.

# CHAPTER 8

# NOBILITY'S RULE

Royal identity engenders nobility. Knowing who you are transforms how you behave. People who know they are kings will live as kings. So how should kings then live? This question has been pondered deeply by philosophers since time immemorial. Ancient Greeks and Romans fussed over the question of kingly character and developed a long record of arguments over the true meaning of "nobility."

These days there are two widely used meanings of nobility:

(1) Social rank of superiority over others. In medieval society, the nobility was the aristocratic class just under the royal class, the king and his family, and just over the peasant class who served the nobility. This meaning of nobility is rooted in the fallen hierarchicalism that became entrenched due to sin.

(2) Nobility is also "having or showing fine personal qualities or high moral principles and ideals; of excellent or superior quality."[1]

If you've been tracing the thread of my remarks, then you know that I adamantly reject the first meaning of "social rank of superiority" with its inherent supremacy. Hands down, I fully reject that twisted sense of nobility. That's the wrong kingdom. But the second meaning? Now, that one fascinates me. Because the revelation of royal identity totally

[1] New Oxford American Dictionary

transforms how we see ourselves and others. Royal identity produces "fine personal qualities or high moral principles and ideals; of excellent or superior quality."

Look at Peter's powerful statement again where he extols our display of God's "excellencies":

> *But you are a chosen race, a royal priesthood, a holy nation, a people for God's own possession, so that you may proclaim the excellencies of Him who has called you out of darkness into His marvelous light. (1 Peter 2:9)*

Father God chose us in Christ to be kings and priests—literally, kingly priests—who would display His excellency, the excellency of heaven into earth. By restoring our royal identity, God unleashes our kingly nature into the world. The Kingdom of God flows into the world through our kingly behavior. By living and serving as kings in the world, the Kingdom of Heaven takes root in the nations and global culture is transformed. Kingly people unleash the Kingdom.

> ***Noble men and women living in perfect unity are God's strategy for transforming the nations.***

Gender equality is an expression of heaven's excellence. When the world sees redeemed men and women living out love for one another without any attempt to subjugate each other, then the glory of God manifest in image-bearing humans fills the earth. I am not exaggerating one wisp of a hair when I say that noble men and women living in perfect unity are God's strategy for transforming the nations.

Nobility captures the imagination of fallen people. Nobility inspires nobility. When we see people behaving nobly, when we see them rising above the gravitational pull of a fallen world—like a majestic hot air balloon floating gently above the clouds—we can't help but stare. Our eye is drawn upward toward higher, better possibilities. This is why we love books, music and movies that celebrate heroes who prove exceptional deeds are possible for average people.

Who can forget Sydney Carton in Dickens' *A Tale of Two Cities* approaching the tumbril with head held high: "It is a far, far better thing that I do, than I have ever done; it is a far, far better rest that I go to than I have ever known." What nobility! From tales of heroism on the *Titanic* to examples of heart-wrenching self-sacrifice when the towers fell on 9/11 to William Wallace leading the Scots—on and on—we are all inspired by people who emerge from obscurity into renown, from fear into courage, from normalcy into nobility.

Nobility reminds us that we were created for something better than sin and death. Nobility strikes a resonant chord in our heart, an echo of how we were made before we believed satan's lies and unleashed hell on the world. Nobility reminds us that we were created to be kingly priests administrating dominion in partnership with our Creator. Nobility highlights for one glorious moment that exceptional behavior was never meant to be the exception.

Holy Spirit tunes in to that inner resonance, that innate longing for greatness and glory, and harnesses our "nobility-attraction" to draw yearning hearts to the Kingdom. This is how the Kingdom comes. Jesus said that our "good works" will attract unbelievers to the Father:

> *Let your light shine before men in such a way that they may see your good works, and glorify your Father who is in heaven. (Matthew 5:16)*

Peter said much the same thing:

> *Keep your behavior excellent among the Gentiles, so that in the thing in which they slander you as evildoers, they may because of your good deeds, as they observe them, glorify God in the day of visitation. (1 Peter 2:12)*

The call to nobility calls us back to our royal identity.

## *Noblesse Oblige*

We know instinctively that nobility doesn't come easily to fallen people. Those who achieve nobility reach for it. Even those born into noble status must intentionally pursue nobility. It doesn't happen accidentally. In the Middle Ages, nobles were challenged to use their high rank to make the world a better place. It was assumed that noble birth did not guarantee noble behavior. Children born into privilege had to be trained to use their privilege to serve others.

The idea that people born into noble birth have an obligation to serve those less fortunate was captured in the French phrase, "noblesse oblige." As Longfellow put it, "Noble by birth, yet nobler by great deeds."[2] Noblesse oblige was rooted in Jesus' statement, "To whom much is given, much is required" (Luke 12:48). As much as we resist the hierarchicalism of medieval society, yet we must acknowledge that a sincere and systemic attempt was made to call nobles to true nobility. With mixed success, I'm sure.

Nobility does require serious, sustained effort. Yet the pursuit of nobility in the Kingdom is quite different from the world. In the world, nobility is taught through daily discipline. Just keep training the young squire, and he'll get it eventually. In the world, good behavior is "tacked on" from the outside, imposed through external pressure. In the Kingdom, nobility flows from our transformed nature rebirthed in Christ. Kingdom nobility also requires serious, sustained effort, but the effort is the effort of the Holy Spirit

---

[2] Henry Wadsworth Longfellow, *Tales of a Wayside Inn* (1863-1874), Part III. The Student's Tale. Emma and Eginhard, line 82

within us, the power of grace habituating righteousness through fellowship with the Father.

It's important that our call for nobility does not become another form of "works-righteousness," the attempt by humans once more to become godlike by eating of the Tree of Knowledge. No way. Our righteousness comes from the faithfulness of Christ, both His faithfulness *for* us at the cross and His faithfulness *in* us through the indwelling power of the Holy Spirit. Our nobility is the nobility of King Jesus flowing through us.

Nobility is natural for believers. We have been *made* kingly priests by the power of the Holy Spirit. Here's how John put it in Revelation 1:

> *To Him who loves us and released us from our sins by His blood—and He has made us to be a kingdom, priests to His God and Father—to Him be the glory and the dominion forever and ever. Amen. (Revelation 1:5–6)*

Jesus *made* us to be kingly priests. He shaped us, formed us, called us, transformed us. Through the power of the Holy Spirit, our nature is transformed, and we gracefully, effortlessly produce the characteristics of nobility—which Paul describes as "the fruit of the Spirit"—as we rest in Him. There's the paradox: we produce through rest. By the grace of God, nobility is natural for us.

Nobility in the Kingdom flows out of a transformed character, a regenerated heart. As we discover our royal identity in Christ, we are reformed into His image. Then His nature blossoms in us and starts bearing fruit that manifests noble behavior. Kingdom nobility is rooted in love.

## *Nobility: A New Way of Leading*

Nobility becomes a new way of leading. Though we reject the hierarchicalism of medieval nobility, yet we do believe in a

Spirit-filled noblesse oblige. "To whom much is given, much is required." We do believe that Kingdom leaders have a call to serve for the benefit of God's people, just not in a patronizing, arrogant way. Being a king in the world's system looks like being in charge, in control, exploiting the people below you in the hierarchy to prop up your personal success. But being a king in the Kingdom of God looks quite different. It looks like serving in love for the good of others. It's a Spirit-filled noblesse oblige.

Just because we reject hierarchicalism does not mean that we reject leadership. Not at all. The Kingdom of God has structure, shape and form. But the structure exists for the good of the people it serves, not for the aggrandizement of the people who lead. There's nothing wrong with order. And there's nothing wrong with structure. As mentioned before, your spinal cord brings structure to the body. But the purpose of the spinal cord is to bring life to the body, not for the body to bring life to the spinal cord. So it is with the Body of Christ.

And what makes Kingdom leadership possible without reverting to a pyramid structure, a wrong-kingdom-hierarchy, is the nobility of character within its leaders. This is why so many churches and ministries become corrupt: the leaders lack nobility of character.

Noblesse oblige requires leaders to use their gifts and callings to serve the people around them. Their resources are not meant to be hoarded, but rather to be developed for the good of all. As Peter phrased it so powerfully,

> *Therefore, I exhort the elders among you, as your fellow elder and witness of the sufferings of Christ, and a partaker also of the glory that is to be revealed, shepherd the flock of God among you, exercising oversight not under compulsion, but voluntarily, according to the will of God;*

> *and not for sordid gain, but with eagerness; nor yet as lording it over those allotted to your charge, but proving to be examples to the flock.*
>
> *And when the Chief Shepherd appears, you will receive the unfading crown of glory. You younger men, likewise, be subject to your elders; and all of you, clothe yourselves with humility toward one another, for God is opposed to the proud, but gives grace to the humble. Therefore humble yourselves under the mighty hand of God, that He may exalt you at the proper time. (1 Peter 5:1–6)*

Kingdom leaders serve without compulsion, not for "sordid gain," and they do not "lord" themselves over other believers. As the KJV renders it, "Neither as being lords over God's heritage." This is exactly opposite of the "gentile" leadership Jesus warned against:

> ***Since the Kingdom of God is a love-based Kingdom, Kingdom leaders can only lead through love, for love and to love.***

> *And He said to them, "The kings of the Gentiles lord it over them; and those who have authority over them are called 'Benefactors.' But it is not this way with you, but the one who is the greatest among you must become like the youngest, and the leader like the servant." (Luke 22:25–26)*

A leader leads, and when you are a Kingdom leader, you must lead people to the Kingdom and to Kingdom values. Since the Kingdom of God is a love-based Kingdom, Kingdom leaders can only lead through love, for love and to love. In fact, if we could abbreviate noblesse oblige in the Kingdom, we would spell it l-o-v-e.

Whatever is in us will come out. They used to say in England that some people are so aristocratic that if you cut them, they would bleed blue. People should be able to say of us that if they cut us, we will bleed love. One of my daughter's favorite expressions is, "Your cup got bumped," which means that something just happened that made whatever is in you come sloshing out. The English also used to say of the nobility, "Breeding will tell." If you are noble, it will come out in times of great pressure. Who we are inside manifests eventually.

Jesus said it like this:

> *For the mouth speaks out of that which fills the heart. The good man brings out of his good treasure what is good; and the evil man brings out of his evil treasure what is evil. (Matthew 12:34–35)*

Remember, the Kingdom of heaven is *within* you. The only way to spread the Kingdom throughout the world is to get it flowing out of you and me. There is no other "spigot" for the Kingdom. Heaven flows like a river from our belly—our innermost being—and comes out our mouth, hands and feet. If we want to see culture transformed into the nobility of heaven, then we must develop a noble heart that flows out as noble leadership through loving service.

What does Spirit-filled noblesse oblige look like? It looks like the "extra mile" we talked about earlier. My husband, Gregory, has such a deep conviction about going the extra mile that he named a ministry he once led, "Extra Mile Ministries." The "extra mile" mentality comes from a noble mindset. Going the extra mile means that, no matter what people ask of you, no matter what they demand of you, you lead with love. Sometimes love means you say no, but the no still comes from love, not rejection.

And that's how nobles rule. That's how they respond. Nobles become powerful through love. The kingdom of darkness tries to enslave us, to control us, by demanding that we walk a mile. But when we freely agree and cheerfully offer to go the extra mile, the compulsion of evil is broken. How can I be forced to do what I willingly choose to do? Love says, "I'm glad to serve you even more than you require." Love says, "I will lay down my life for you." Love is noblesse oblige.

God's Kingdom is an upside down kingdom. If you desire to be the greatest in God's Kingdom, you must become the least. And your least-ness cannot be a conniving sleight of hand that fakes humility to achieve superiority. No, it means you come underneath others with genuine compassion and lift them up.

One of my favorite works of art is a prophetic painting that I purchased because of how well it captures this message. The painting depicts two dancers, a male and female, and the man is lifting the woman up as she whirls in pure delight. He is "leading" her, but his leadership supports and releases her to express her God-given creativity. In fact, as we shall see in Book 3, this painting perfectly captures the essence of biblical "headship."

The image also perfectly captures noblesse oblige. Noble kings rule by serving, by lifting people up to be released. Noble kings live their lives for the good of those within their influence, within their domain. Noble kings ride through their kingdom to see what the people need. Noble kings long to see how they can empower the people to become all that God intended them to be. Noble kings are not driven by a lust for power that exploits vulnerable people.

A noble king does not ride out to see what he or she can strip from helpless subjects by overtaxing them. A noble king is not driven to fill his or her coffers just to make himself even more wealthy at their expense. A noble king knows that when he or she does that, the people are impoverished, which impoverishes his or her own kingdom.

A noble king understands the cycle of blessing. The more the people are blessed, the more the kingdom is blessed. It becomes circular. It's just the way the Kingdom works—the more you give away, the more you get. So the more a noble king gives away, the more his or her kingdom prospers. It's a Kingdom principle.

That's how we lead. That's how we rule. That's how we govern in the Kingdom of heaven. We rule through love. It may be counterintuitive, but it's how the Kingdom comes. *Noblesse oblige.*

# CHAPTER 9

# TAKING DOMINION

The Kingdom of God operates in a way that makes chauvinism impossible. Because the Kingdom operates from within the noble human heart transformed by love, wherever chauvinism, supremacy and misogyny are present *the Kingdom is not*. The Kingdom of God is spiritual. The Kingdom of God is not an external, objective reality that can be held in your hands, weighed in a box or measured in a frame. The Kingdom of God impacts and transforms external reality, but the Kingdom itself is Spirit.

Did you get that?

The Kingdom impacts the material world, but it cannot be contained by it. And it cannot be identified with it. The Kingdom of God is not a place, a building or an organization. So any institution, program or social group that functions as a pyramid that elevates one person over another *in that moment* is not the Kingdom of God. This is how a Church, family or business can become the wrong kingdom in an instant. The Kingdom of God is present only when people live in harmony with the Holy Spirit and unleash the Kingdom into the world. The Kingdom has no other source in the world than Spirit-filled people.

As Paul said, "The kingdom of God is not eating and drinking, but righteousness and peace and joy in the Holy Spirit" (Romans 14:17). Do you see how significant that really is? Whatever is not Holy Spirit-powered is the wrong kingdom.

This is why the Kingdom of God cannot be unleashed by slightly adjusting existing power structures. We cannot redeem Egypt's pyramids and Babel's ziggurats. They must be razed to the ground! We cannot simply take the sign down on evil systems and re-christen them as the Kingdom of God. This is exactly what happened when the Church was institutionalized after Constantine. The politicized Church swept into every part of the Roman Empire "baptizing" paganism into the Christian religion. But it was the wrong kingdom. It was a political conversion, not a heart conversion. And it has borne the terrible fruit of evil in every generation since. It is a crying shame that so much hostility, perversion and greed has marched through the earth under the banner of Christendom. It is a travesty. And it is time to stop it.

All this applies specifically to the quest for equality. The only way to end male supremacy is to unleash the Kingdom of God. And the only way to unleash the Kingdom of God is to invite Holy Spirit to flood our hearts and pour out of us into every corner of the earth. The dominion of King Jesus is extended through us. His domain is first you and me, in our sanctified hearts. And as He is enthroned in you and me, His throne advances in every hamlet, village, city and nation where we live, work and play.

This is why a renewed royal identity that produces Spirit-filled nobility is such a big deal. We can rush around the planet "fixing" people by shaming them into compliance to our new equality-driven ideals. We can try to advance the Kingdom through "cancel culture." But that's shame-based, and shame is the wrong kingdom. Shame puts people down. (Sanctimony is its mirror-opposite. Both are the wrong kingdom.)

We can "feminize" every human structure on the planet and socialize little boys and girls with our new vision of equality—nay, equity!—but the hostility between men and women is sublimated perforce, creating an inevitable backlash. Men will not just ride the supremacy seesaw down to the other side as we flip from male domination to female domination. Men will fight back! Threatened humans always fight back.

We can have a million more "Me, Too" campaigns, but until the hearts of men and women are transformed, we will repeatedly revert back to our fallen state. This is why equality between men and women is *only possible as we unleash the Kingdom*. There is no other way.

## *The Kingdom Transforms the World*

> ***The fruit that the Kingdom bears is dominion.***

The Kingdom of God is unleashed through the regenerated human heart, but it does not end there. Just as much as we emphasize the internalization of the Kingdom—it doesn't take root in the world any other way!—we must also emphasize its externalization. We must neither over-materialize nor over-spiritualize the Kingdom. It takes root in the heart and bears fruit in the earth.

The fruit that the Kingdom bears is dominion. The Kingdom of God is God's domain. Dominion is the governance exercised within that domain. God's domain includes heaven and earth, for "heaven is My throne and the earth is My footstool " (Isaiah 66:1). But here's the clincher: God delegated to humans dominion over the earth. God, the King of all creation, made humans kings over the earth. He gave us dominion.

God never took that dominion away. Even when satan invaded the earth as a serpent and deceived humans into aligning their authority with him, God did not revoke human dominion. In fact, the reason the serpent took such pains to beguile Adam and Eve was because he knew that dominion had been given to humans. In order to gain a foothold in the earth, the serpent had to usurp authority from humans. As Bill Johnson often says, satan has power but no authority. He can only get authority from those who have it, and that's you and me.

Psalm 8, which was written about humans after the Fall, makes it clear: human dominion was never revoked. This is why Jesus, God the Son, came *as a human* to restore the Kingdom of God within the earth, the realm assigned by God the Father to humans. As a human, Jesus was qualified to represent humans. When Jesus died, rose again and ascended, He realigned human authority with the Father's authority. Jesus declared, "All authority has been given to Me in heaven and on earth" (Matthew 28:18). The authority given to Adam and squandered in the Fall was now fully transferred to King Jesus.

Now the call of the gospel of the Kingdom goes out to every human on the planet: "Believe on Christ—which means quite literally to transfer your allegiance to Christ as King—and be born again into the new humanity, become loyal citizens of heaven's rule on earth and expand the domain of King Jesus by implementing Kingdom authority through loving service in your own assigned area of influence."

When we are saved, we transfer kingdoms. As Paul put it in Colossians 1:

> *For He rescued us from the domain of darkness, and transferred us to the kingdom of His beloved Son. (Colossians 1:13)*

We are transferred to a new Kingdom. We are transferred from "the domain of darkness," which is the kingdom of satan, to "the Kingdom of our Lord and of His Christ" (Revelation 11:15). The domain of darkness was the domain of Adam that humans collaborated with the power of the evil one. Adam and Eve believed the enemy's lies and thus invited him into their house. Satan gained control of the earth through deluded human permission.

As John said, "The whole world lies in the power of the evil one" (1 John 5:19), but then he goes on to say:

> *And we know that the Son of God has come, and has given us understanding so that we may know Him who is true; and we are in Him who is true, in His Son Jesus Christ. This is the true God and eternal life. (1 John 5:20)*

Jesus came to tell us the truth, to break the power of the lie that bewitched us. Jesus came to give us *understanding*. He came so we could know Him, for He *is* The Truth, and that we would discover our true royal identity in Him. Our identity—our godlikeness—is not found outside Him in some "apple," in some external, religious, political or social performance. No! Our true identity is found in The Truth, Jesus Christ.

In His resurrection and ascension, Jesus received the authority once given to Adam and tragically ensnared by the evil one. (Matthew 28:18) At the cross, God stripped the evil powers that had exploited human authority. He "disarmed the rulers and authorities," and "He made a public display of them, having triumphed over them through Him" (Colossians 2:15). God nailed the law to the cross thus canceling any legal, prosecutorial right the evil one had to condemn the human race. Since the power of sin lay within the condemnation of the law (1 Corinthians 15:56), Jesus broke the power of sin by fulfilling the law in His innocent death on the cursed tree.

*Christ redeemed us from the curse of the Law, having become a curse for us—for it is written, "Cursed is everyone who hangs on a tree." (Galatians 3:13)*

Through Jesus' obedience, the dominion of humans, which had never been revoked, was now realigned in submission to the Father. Adam's "treaty" with death was annulled. The original creation mandate to have dominion was still in force, but now it included the new creation mandate for the rescue and restoration of a fallen world. It was time to "rebuild the ancient ruins, raise up the former devastations and repair the ruined cities, the desolations of many generations" (Isaiah 61:4). Jesus, when quoting Isaiah 61 during His Sabbath message in Nazareth, declared implicitly that rebuilding ruined cities is why "the Spirit of the Lord [was] upon [Him]" (Luke 4:18). Jesus came "to destroy the works of the devil" (1 John 3:8) and to restore Kingdom dominion.

Listen close in Luke's account of Christ's final moments with His disciples and you will hear distinct echoes of the blessing in Genesis 1:28, the original creation mandate:

*And He led them out as far as Bethany, and He lifted up His hands and blessed them. While He was blessing them, He parted from them and was carried up into heaven. (Luke 24:50–51)*

Jesus "blessed them" just like God did originally in the garden. In fact, there was a "blessing scene" each time God sent forth His people into a covenant assignment in the earth: God blessed Noah, God blessed Abraham, God blessed Israel, God blessed David, God blessed Solomon—and now, Jesus blessed the disciples. Luke's account was deliberately evocative of all the commissioning scenes in Scripture. God blessed His covenant people to go out and take dominion in the earth. It is exactly what Jesus did when He commissioned His disciples to go and preach the gospel of the Kingdom.

Here's how Matthew described Jesus' commission to His disciples just before the blessing scene in Luke 24:

> *But the eleven disciples proceeded to Galilee, to the mountain which Jesus had designated. When they saw Him, they worshiped Him; but some were doubtful. And Jesus came up and spoke to them, saying, "All authority has been given to Me in heaven and on earth.*
>
> *"Go therefore and make disciples of all the nations, baptizing them in the name of the Father and the Son and the Holy Spirit, teaching them to observe all that I commanded you; and lo, I am with you always, even to the end of the age." (Matthew 28:16–20)*

**The internalization of the Kingdom taking root in the heart becomes the externalization of the Kingdom bearing fruit in the world.**

Can you see Luke's version flowing together with Matthew's? Luke is careful to frame the commission in terms of the original creation mandate, in terms of covenantal blessing. In Matthew, Jesus gathered with His disciples on the mountain and told them to "Go, disciple the nations." And then in Luke, He "blessed them" to fulfill the task. With Luke's echo of Eden, the dominion mandate is connected implicitly to the discipling mandate. And the discipling mandate is all about training disciples to take dominion.

This is where the *internalization* of the Kingdom taking root in the heart becomes the *externalization* of the Kingdom bearing fruit in the world. The original creation mandate to take dominion over the earth is now fulfilled by discipling the nations. The mandate hasn't changed. We must still "be fruitful and multiply, and fill the earth, and subdue it; and rule." But now, thanks to the cross of Jesus and the outpouring of the Holy Spirit, our hearts are prepared for the task. Because Holy Spirit disciples the heart, the Church can disciple the nations. In a nutshell, discipling the nations means to disciple people for dominion.

### *Disciple All the Nations*

You've probably noticed that I keep quoting Jesus' command in Matthew 28:19 as "disciple the nations" rather than "make disciples of all the nations" as the NASB renders it. Here's why:

The Greek phrase is "*matheteusate panta ta ethne,*" which is literally "disciple all the people groups." The imperative command here is "disciple" and it is quite forceful, something like, "Go, therefore. *DISCIPLE!*" It's almost as if Jesus shouts it. Not quite, but almost.

The rest of the phrase is also interesting. Who must we disciple? "*Panta ta ethne.*" Literally, "all the people groups." All the "people groups" are usually seen as nations, though it includes ethnic groups within nations. This is important because the command to disciple the nations is bigger than we think. It's more than just getting the gospel across geopolitical borders, planting our flag and declaring that the Kingdom has now arrived in one more nation. (Check the box: one more nation down, how many more to go?) No, the gospel is meant to take root and flourish in "every tribe and tongue and people and nation" (Revelation 5:9).

It also means much more than just discipling a few people within the people groups. Jesus envisions whole people groups being discipled. Jesus' commission entails more than just individual dominion. Dominion is not complete until we "multiply, fill up the earth and subdue it." Discipling the nations is much more than just cherry-picking a few disciples out of each nation as a representative sample. Discipling the nations actually means pervading the nations with the gospel so deeply that "all the *ethne*" bow before Christ as King.

The Old Testament prophets, the New Testament writers, and most of all Jesus Himself, teach us to expect the widespread victory of Christ's Kingdom over the hostile powers insomuch that the nations of the earth will come to worship Jesus as Lord. Isaiah 61:1-4, the passage we referenced above, is one of the most vivid examples of that expectation. Isaiah 61 shows both the *internalization* and the *externalization* of the Kingdom. Look close:

> *The Spirit of the Lord God is upon me, because the Lord has anointed me to bring good news to the afflicted; He has sent me to bind up the brokenhearted, to proclaim liberty to captives and freedom to prisoners; to proclaim the favorable year of the Lord and the day of vengeance of our God; to comfort all who mourn, to grant those who mourn in Zion, giving them a garland instead of ashes, the oil of gladness instead of mourning, the mantle of praise instead of a spirit of fainting. (Isaiah 61:1-3a)*

Did you see the *internalization* of the Kingdom here? The gospel impacts the individual: the afflicted, the broken-hearted, the captives, the prisoners and the mourners. This is how the Kingdom takes root in the world. It brings personal transformation through regeneration of the heart.

But what happens in the heart doesn't stay in the heart. (Unlike Vegas.) The transformation of the heart produces transformation of behavior. And when enough people have been converted to Christ, society cannot help but be deeply impacted. How can we expect to change people without changing the world? No way.

Those who emphasize a privatized gospel are missing the point. Those who are transformed by King Jesus are called by King Jesus to mediate His love into the world through Kingdom influence. As Isaiah goes on to proclaim,

> *So they will be called oaks of righteousness, the planting of the Lord, that He may be glorified. (Isaiah 61:3b)*

Transformed people will be called "oaks of righteousness." And they will bear lasting fruit so that God may be glorified, so that "all the earth will be filled with the glory of the Lord" (Numbers 14:21). God's strategy for filling the earth with His glory is "Christ in you, the hope of glory" (Colossians 1:27). And, as transformed people bear fruit in all nations, this is what "discipled-for-dominion" will look like:

> ***The internal reality of the Kingdom, the royal identity that becomes deep-seated nobility, becomes the external reality of a transformed world.***

> *Then they will rebuild the ancient ruins, they will raise up the former devastations; and they will repair the ruined cities, the desolations of many generations. (Isaiah 61:4)*

As the afflicted, the broken-hearted, the captives, the prisoners and the mourners all become born again, baptized disciples of Jesus, they start living out the gospel of the Kingdom in the world. The Kingdom flows from their heart into their relationships, their family, their vocation, their neighborhoods, everywhere they go. The *internal* reality of the Kingdom, the royal identity that becomes deep-seated nobility, becomes the *external* reality of a transformed world.

Another powerful promise of global dominion is the blessing of Abraham. (Genesis 12:1-3) The blessing of Abraham starts in the transformed heart, but then flows out to transformed nations. As Peter preached in Acts 3,

> *And likewise, all the prophets who have spoken, from Samuel and his successors onward, also announced these days. It is you who are the sons of the prophets and of the covenant which God made with your fathers, saying to Abraham, "And in your seed all the families of the earth shall be blessed." For you first, God raised up His Servant and sent Him to bless you by turning every one of you from your wicked ways. (Acts 3:24–26)*

Did you catch the progression? God raised up Jesus to bless us "by turning every one of [us] from [our] wicked ways," and through this blessing salvation will flow out until "all the families of the earth shall be blessed." As the blessing of Abraham transforms people, society is transformed. As society is transformed, culture is transformed.

The idea that the gospel of the Kingdom entails the transformation of culture is described by many as "the Seven Mountain Revelation," which is a way of describing metaphorically the spheres of influence within culture. Though different teachers use varying names for the "mountains," the groupings generally go something like:

- Government
- Education
- Science
- Arts and Media
- Religion
- Family
- Business

The first teachings on this idea were presented by Loren Cunningham and Bill Bright in 1975 after both men met and discovered that each had independently received a revelation about the seven mountains of culture. More recently, Lance Wallnau and Johnny Enlow have been two of the most vocal "Seven Mountains" proponents, along with many others.

The idea is that there are seven primary areas of culture, each with its own demonic principality that rules each mountain illegally in defiance of Christ's authority. Each spiritual strongman must be expelled from the mountain so that Christian leaders can ascend to the highest levels of influence. Not control, but loving influence. Every believer is given Kingdom assignments within these mountains, and through them, King Jesus will unleash His Kingdom into each mountain and eventually rule them all.

Some people get nervous at this level of expectation for Kingdom victory in this present world prior to the Second Coming. Some feel it is a form of triumphalism, or even implicit universalism. But it's really not. Never do the prophets, Jesus or any of His apostles ever predict that every human on the planet will be saved. And never is the Kingdom triumphalistic. *That's the point we're presently making: the Kingdom cannot be forced on anyone!* People will always be free to say no to Christ. Love always offers a choice, remember?

But the prophets, Jesus and the apostles *do* predict that all the nations will come to worship the one true God. And they predict that the enemies of Christ—the evil powers that dominate the earth through lies—will be subdued under His feet before Jesus returns. (1 Corinthians 15) They do predict that earthly culture will be suffused with "the knowledge of the glory of the Lord" (Habakkuk 2:14). The love of Christ will so thoroughly permeate the earth that believers will become "a great multitude which no one could count, from every nation and all tribes and peoples and tongues" (Revelation 7:9). Can you imagine the cultural impact of a redeemed multitude that vast?

So, while I agree that we are never taught to expect that every human on the planet will come to faith in Christ, I still strongly assert that we should expect that the true worship of Christ will become the prevailing pattern of life for family, church, business, government, education, media—on and on.

How do we know this is true? First of all, because God the Father promised Jesus the nations—not just a few select people within the nations!—as His inheritance:

> *I will surely tell of the decree of the Lord: He said to Me, "You are My Son, today I have begotten You. Ask of Me, and I will surely give the nations as Your inheritance, and the very ends of the earth as Your possession. (Psalm 2:7–8)*

Paul preached boldly in Acts 13 that God's promise to Christ in Psalm 2 was already being fulfilled in the Church:

> *And we preach to you the good news of the promise made to the fathers, that God has fulfilled this promise to our children in that He raised up Jesus, as it is also written in the second Psalm, "You are My Son; today I have begotten You." (Acts 13:32-33)*

Did you get that? God has fulfilled to our children the Psalm 2 promise made to the fathers, and the seal of this promise was Christ's resurrection from the dead. In other words, the fact that God raised Jesus from the dead *guarantees* that God has given all nations to Jesus, Israel's Messiah, as His inheritance. How could Jesus ever doubt His inheritance? God raised Jesus from the dead as proof of His faithfulness.

Then, as further proof, Jesus' Father gave Him "the promise of the Father," the Holy Spirit, as the earnest of Christ's inheritance.

> *Therefore having been exalted to the right hand of God, and having received from the Father the promise of the Holy Spirit, He has poured forth this which you both see and hear. (Acts 2:33)*

The outpouring of the Spirit was the Father's down payment on "the *eschaton*," the age to come. By pouring out the Holy Spirit, Father God guaranteed that the future could not fail—for it was already present! The final outcome is not in question.

Moreover, when Father God poured out the Spirit of the age to come into the middle of history, He gathered the Church as the first-fruits of a global harvest. (James 1:18; Revelation 14:4) First century believers saw themselves as the initial harvest that proclaimed the certainty of the harvest to come.

Why do we believe then that Jesus will inevitably inherit the nations? Because of His resurrection, His ascension and enthronement, the outpouring of the Holy Spirit and the formation of the Church into Christ's resurrected body. The Kingdom cannot fail because the victory is already won.

In Matthew 13, Jesus compared the Kingdom to yeast that permeates the whole lump of dough. *This is what the Kingdom is like*. It pervades the earth through regenerated people until all the nations bow before Christ as King. In the same chapter, Jesus also compared the Kingdom to a mustard seed that begins so small and insignificant but then grows into a tree large enough for birds to build nests in its branches.

With both examples, the yeast and the mustard seed, Jesus teaches us something powerful about the Kingdom: it starts small but eventually grows large and permeates the whole. This both shows the *manner* in which the Kingdom comes and the *extent* of its success. The Kingdom comes *slowly* but *surely*.

The victory of Christ's Kingdom must never be reduced to only a privatized, personal experience of salvation. Just because the Kingdom is not "of this world" (John 18:36) does not mean it has no impact on the world. When Jesus said His Kingdom is not "of this world," He simply meant the Kingdom comes into the world from heaven. His Kingdom does not arise from within the world's system. But He never meant that the Kingdom would dwell privately within our heart and make no external impact on the world.

Moreover, the Kingdom must not be postponed until after Jesus comes again. Jesus made it clear that the Kingdom would not "appear immediately" (Luke 19:11), neither at His First Advent in the first century nor at His Second Advent at the end of history. We should not be surprised that it takes a long time—twenty centuries so far!—for the Kingdom to fully take root among all the nations.

> ***The victory of Christ's Kingdom must never be reduced to only a privatized, personal experience of salvation.***

## *Healed People, Healed World*

Jesus came to earth to realign human dominion with heaven. At the cross, Jesus broke the power of sin and death that enslaved the human race. In His burial, Jesus descended into the heart of hell and stripped the enemy of "the power of death" (Hebrews 2:14). Jesus took "the keys of death and of Hades" (Revelation 1:18). Then Jesus ascended into heaven and was crowned as King of all creation. Next, He received the promise of the Father, the Holy Spirit, and came to dwell within believers as the Spirit of Kingship. Remember, the Kingdom of God is "righteousness, peace and joy *in the Holy Spirit*" (Romans 14:17).

By filling believers with the power of the Holy Spirit, King Jesus empowers us to be kings. We can now succeed where Adam failed because King Jesus is the "last Adam" (1 Corinthians 15:45) and He lives within us. "The first man is from the earth, earthy; the second man is from heaven" (1 Corinthians 15:47). We can bring heaven to earth because we have heaven living within us. We have the Spirit of the victorious Jesus living in us. We have the Spirit of a new, victorious humanity. We are new creation.

As Paul put it, "The last Adam became a life-giving spirit" (1 Corinthians 15:45). We were born the first time into Adam, but we are born the second time into Christ. As Jesus said, we must be born again "of water and Spirit" so that we may "see" and "enter" the Kingdom. (John 3:3, 5) Those born in Adam cannot enter the Kingdom of God, for as Jesus said:

> *That which is born of the flesh is flesh, and that which is born of the Spirit is spirit. (John 3:6)*

And Paul adds:

> *Now I say this, brethren, that flesh and blood cannot inherit the kingdom of God. (1 Corinthians 15:50)*

The Kingdom is in the Holy Spirit, which means unregenerate humans cannot enter or even see the Kingdom. This is why I keep emphasizing that the Kingdom of God cannot come in the earth apart from transformed hearts. Regeneration is *re-genesis*. When we are born again, the Spirit of the living Christ reforms and recreates us from the inside out. Then new creation flows out of us into the world around us.

Saved people are Kingdom people. We advance the Kingdom because the always-advancing King of kings lives within us. As Isaiah proclaimed, "There will be no end to the increase of His government or of peace" (Isaiah 9:7). The increasing victory of Christ's Kingdom is increasing within us. As we grow personally in the image of heaven, we bear that image into the world around us. As Paul said, "Just as we have borne the image of the earthy, we will also bear the image of the heavenly" (1 Corinthians 15:49).

This is how we become the embodied answer to the prayer, "Your will be done on earth as it is in heaven" (Matthew 6:10). The will of God will not fall out of the sky. And it will not happen while we stand by and watch. No, God's will is done through you and me. The victory of Christ is not just a historical fact that we can observe objectively and applaud. The victory of Jesus is living within us now. We are kingly because the King resides within our heart. Individually and collectively, we are His temple, His palace.

Think back to Isaiah 61. The Spirit of the Lord God came upon Jesus so He could bring good news to fallen people. By healing the afflicted, binding up the brokenhearted, liberating the captives, freeing the prisoners and comforting the mourners, Jesus unleashed the Kingdom of God in their hearts. Jesus did not bypass people. He did not look for shortcuts. He did not seek political, military, economic or even religious solutions to world problems. Jesus did not see people as expendable or ancillary to His task. People were the center of His redemptive strategy. Jesus knew that the only solution to world problems was redeemed people. The only way to save the world is to save people. Then saved people will save the world.

Notice that Jesus didn't arrive on Planet Earth with a plan to rebuild desolated cities. He didn't come with strategies to feed the hungry, clothe the naked, house the homeless, provide clean water, dispense free medicine, advocate for justice, though *all those things matter deeply to Him*. But Jesus came with a plan to save people, to fill them with the Holy Spirit, so that Father God could partner with people for solutions for the world's most intractable problems.

Here's how saved people save the world. When the Holy Spirit fills a believer, He opens up a river of life within our "belly," which is the deepest part of the human spirit. As Jesus put it:

> *Now on the last day, the great day of the feast, Jesus stood and cried out, saying, "If anyone is thirsty, let him come to Me and drink. He who believes in Me, as the Scripture said, 'From his innermost being will flow rivers of living water.'" But this He spoke of the Spirit, whom those who believed in Him were to receive; for the Spirit was not yet given, because Jesus was not yet glorified. (John 7:37–39)*

> ***Jesus came with a plan to save people, to fill them with the Holy Spirit, so that Father God could partner with people for solutions for the world's most intractable problems.***

The river of living water that springs from our "innermost being" flows from our human spirit into our soul, which is our center of consciousness, our mind, will and emotions. Holy Spirit starts the process of healing our emotions, our will and our mind. This is what so many call "inner healing," where Holy Spirit repairs the fragmented human soul. Every human born into a fallen world has shattered bits and pieces of their soul that must be healed in order for them to be fully restored in the image of God. Isaiah 61:1 calls this being "brokenhearted." In extreme cases, psychiatrists call it "dissociation." We are disintegrated because of sin, but when Holy Spirit heals us, He reintegrates our emotions, will and mind. He makes us truly free by making us truly whole.

One of the most powerful expressions of inner healing is a transformed mind. The Word of God that dwells in us richly takes our thoughts captive. (2 Corinthians 10:5) Thoughts that once served as slaves to satan's lies are delivered from the stronghold of false mindsets and are delivered to serve the mind of Christ. By the power of the Holy Spirit, our thoughts are no longer "conformed to this world" but are powerfully "transformed by the renewing of [our] mind" (Romans 12:2).

Then, as healing flows out of our spirit and soul, it manifests physically in our body. Our countenance, words and deeds are aligned with the true self we are in Christ. We no longer need to "fake it until we make it." We no longer need to conform to external expectations. We no longer live in the fear of man. We become a truly integrated whole, fully alive in the Spirit and manifesting the image of God in Christ.

As we are made whole—as we learn to relate better to God and who He made us to be in Him—we can better relate to others. Inner healing flows out as healed relationships. If it's true that "hurt people hurt people," then it's also true that "healed people heal people." The change God makes inside us begins to change the world around us. Healing flows through us. Heaven flows through us.

As Holy Spirit heals us, He gives us dominion over our heart. Our heart is the garden we are first given to manage. Just as Adam and Eve were given the Garden of Eden as the prototype of global dominion, so we are given dominion over our heart as the prototype of the dominion assigned to us in the world at large. We cannot exercise dominion in our family, our church or our community if we do not have dominion over our own heart.

Psalm 119:13 says, "Establish my footsteps in your word and do not let any iniquity have dominion over me." We cannot exercise dominion over areas of life where we are enslaved. As Paul said, we are slaves to whatever we obey. (Romans 6:16) Jesus came to break the dominion of iniquity in our life so that we could exercise the dominion He intended at first.

Iniquity wants to control us. In Genesis 4:7, Scripture describes sin as "crouching at the door" like a wild animal ready to devour Cain. That's what sin is like. God does not forbid sin because He's a killjoy or just because He loves arbitrary, made-up rules. He's not power-flexing when He tells you not to sin. He knows the rapacious nature of sin, and He urgently warns against its destructive power. God wants to see you free. He wants to see you empowered. Your Heavenly Father wants to see you happy, prosperous, healthy, alive and kicking the devil's butt! That's why He's furious against sin.

Dominion begins in the heart.

## *Right Kingdom In the Real World*

When the Kingdom takes root in the heart, it bears fruit in the real world. The *internalized* Kingdom manifests as *externalized* Kingdom in very practical ways.

For example, several years ago, someone broke into our vehicle. Gregory called the insurance agency to talk with them about it. As Gregory started to explain what happened, the representative interjected, "Now before you tell me all the details of what happened, I want to tell you that if the truck was in the driveway, then the homeowner's insurance will cover it. That means you will have a much higher deductible because it's one percent of the value of your home. If the truck was parked on the street, then your auto insurance will cover it, which would be a much lower deductible."

Significant pause.

Now, we're talking about a difference of at least a thousand dollars. Out of our pocket. Before we answer the question, consider: it's only three feet difference. Was it here? Or there? In the driveway, or on the street?

Still pausing.

Then the rep asked, "Now where was the truck parked when it was broken into?"

One final pause.

Gregory knew the truck was in the driveway. No question. But it was a thousand dollar difference, and the insurance rep seemed determined to help us save the money even if it meant fudging the story a bit.

Of course, Gregory is honest to the core. And he's "right Kingdom" in every way. So he answered it correctly. "The truck was in the driveway," he replied.

One more final pause.

The representative seemed a bit perplexed by such unusual honesty, but no further comment was made, and we paid the extra thousand dollars. Not easy, but it was the right thing to do. It was the *right Kingdom.*

What difference does it make? All the difference in the world actually. Purity matters. Gregory refused to bring the wrong kingdom into our finances. And by refusing to bring the wrong kingdom into our world, he refused to unleash wrong kingdom into *the* world. Truth was more important than a thousand dollars. Taking dominion starts at home in the inner man. The Kingdom of heaven is located in us. The

Kingdom of God dwells within us. And the Kingdom wants out.

Here's another example:

When Gregory and I first began learning about dominion, I had struggled with a lifelong addiction to tobacco. I had started smoking as a small child and smoked for twenty-five years until about six months after I was saved. Then I remained free from tobacco for about six and a half years. I had put on some weight, and I started thinking that smoking would help me lose it. Opening my mind to those thoughts brought back strong, physical cravings.

Soon after, I went through a really tough season with my son, and my defenses dropped to zero. With no resistance left, I woodenly reached for a pack of cigarettes that he'd left in the house. In one moment, I was fully enslaved again. I became addicted for another four years.

I was so ashamed. Here I was on staff at a church and yet in bondage to a substance I could not control. Due to my shame, I rarely smoked in public, though I did not hide it from those closest to me. In fact, Holy Spirit broke the shame before I was finally and totally free. Though I knew that tobacco itself was not sinful, yet I also knew that the addiction was slavery to the wrong kingdom. But I simply couldn't quit.

A couple of years after falling back into tobacco addiction, I met Gregory, who, oddly enough, is allergic to tobacco. Isn't that wonderfully ironic? As I impatiently waited for many months for him to get interested in me, I thought that I would quit when we started dating. But no. So I promised myself I'd quit when getting engaged. No again. Okay, before we get married. Once more, no.

For more than a year, I tortured myself over quitting. Then I attended a Patricia King conference where I heard a powerful story that unleashed the Kingdom for me. Patricia told the story of being with a ministry team in Cambodia to rescue sex trafficking victims. As they began to take dominion in prayer over the regional spirits that dominate Cambodia through sex trafficking, she saw a vision of the enemy laughing and mocking, "You have no power over spirits you entertain at home!" And Patricia realized that some of the team had issues with spirits of lust or addiction, which undermined their authority over this principality.

When I heard Patricia's story, something rose up inside me. Smoking was no longer a private matter for me. It affected the community around me. It was now a matter of *dominion*. I realized that freedom for me was a matter of unleashing the Kingdom. That simple shift in perspective changed my life. Though I still had occasional lapses, Holy Spirit began to train me to lay cigarettes down as a matter of dominion. He began to show me the authority that I had through the kingly Spirit living inside me. The Kingdom was in me, so I simply needed to let it out.

> ***You cannot rule the enemy if you have no dominion over yourself.***

Dominion changes everything. And the key to taking dominion is to first pursue dominion in your own heart. You cannot rule the enemy if you have no dominion over yourself. Jesus was tempted and yet never sinned because He never surrendered dominion over His heart. He never partnered with satan's lies.

The Book of Proverbs says, "He who rules his spirit [is better] than he who captures a city" (Proverbs 16:32). Do you see where dominion begins? If you rule yourself, then you can take a city. If the Kingdom is unleashed in you, then it will be unleashed in the world. Proverbs also says that "a man who has no control over his spirit" is like "a city without walls" (Proverbs 25:28). And broken-down walls allow the enemy to come in and ravage you at will.

Remember, the enemy has no authority over you unless you give it to him. You have to give him permission to come in. But when you assert the dominion you've been given in Christ over your own heart, then your dominion widens like the ever-expanding Garden of Eden into your family, your work, your community and your world. This is exactly how God unleashes the Kingdom.

### *Dominion and Equality*

The Kingdom of God takes root in our heart and bears fruit in the world. The fruit that the Kingdom bears is dominion. As we gain dominion within the heart, the rule of the Kingdom expands into the world around us. A healed heart produces healed relationships.

And here we are back again, full circle. The Kingdom of God reigning within a healed heart leaves no room for the pride and competition of the world's misogynistic systems. Supremacy over others is wrong kingdom. As healthy dominion works its way out through our relationships, it will work out through gender equality just as it was meant to do in the Garden of Eden. Look at the original dominion mandate again:

> *Then God said, "Let Us make man in Our image, according to Our likeness; and let them rule over the fish of the sea and over the birds of the sky and over the cattle and over all the earth, and over every creeping thing that creeps on the earth."*
>
> *God created man in His own image, in the image of God He created him; male and female He created them.*

> *God blessed them; and God said to them, "Be fruitful and multiply, and fill the earth, and subdue it; and rule over the fish of the sea and over the birds of the sky and over every living thing that moves on the earth." (Genesis 1:26–28)*

Do you see it? All the "thems." I want you to see double for a split second. Male and female together. Dominion is double. There was no way for the male to "be fruitful and multiply" alone. I'd like to see him try it. Male-female division came as a result of the Fall, and Jesus came to fix it.

When dominion takes root in the heart, it breaks the curse and corrects the competitive urge between male and female that sin caused. This is why Jesus came—to bring salvation into the heart, to heal the breach between God and people, between male and female, between humans of all types.

Let me be crystal clear: the Kingdom of God cannot fulfill its dominion mandate as long as women remain subjugated by men. Until we return to the equality of creation before the curse, we will stumble along always falling short of Kingdom dominion. It's time to restore biblical equality and unleash the Kingdom.

# CHAPTER 10

# UNITED WE STAND

In Chapter 1, I said that the move of God that's happening is a *unity through identity* movement that totally reorganizes the structures of human society. By bringing people into the true *identity* for which they were created, the identity hidden for them in Christ before the foundation of the world, Holy Spirit is forging a new human *unity* rooted in the reconciliation purchased for us by Christ at the cross. Our reconciliation with God produces reconciliation with one another. In Chapter 7, we talked more about *unity through identity*, the *royal identity* that comes when we discover who we are as sons of God.

Yet there's more to say on unity. I cannot pound the table enough on this idea: we cannot fulfill our dominion mandate if we remain divided. Satan's strategy is *divide and conquer.* How long will we fall prey to it? I am not exaggerating just because this is my candy-stick topic. The dominion mandate given on the sixth day of creation requires the unity of male and female as the pluripersonal image of God. The Kingdom of God comes into the world through unity. And unity requires equality. If men and women are divided, the image of God is shattered.

The fundamental relationship of all human relationships is male and female. All human life proceeds from this union, and when this union is disrupted, disruption embeds generationally in all other human relationships. And this is why restored unity between men and women has such incredible redemptive potential. As male and female relations are healed, children will grow up in an environment that models and mediates unity.

Recently, at our church, the Kids Team was teaching the children on the love of God. They asked the children the question, "What is love?" All of the young kids without exception answered the question by describing the love between their mothers and fathers—every child without exception. That's astounding. And sobering. Every child's perception of love was shaped by the male-female, husband-wife relationship modeled before them. And that's why getting male-female relationships right will change the world.

## *Emphasis On Unity*

I'm emphasizing unity because the New Testament emphasizes unity. Unity is a big deal in the New Testament. Jesus and the apostles spoke of unity often and highlighted over and over how essential it is to our Kingdom agenda. In fact, one of Jesus' greatest promises was that He would be wherever two or three believers gather in His name. (Matthew 18:20) Unity attracts His presence!

> ***Getting male-female relationships right will change the world.***

One of the most powerful texts on unity is John 17, Jesus' High Priestly prayer that captured His cry for oneness. Unity was such a big deal to Jesus that it was the most urgent thing on His mind just before His crucifixion. His last recorded prayer was all about it. Jesus prayed to His Father that the union between the Father and Son would be experienced and understood by the disciples. Jesus' prayer came to its crescendo with this appeal:

> *Holy Father, keep them in Your name, the name which You have given Me, that they may be one even as We are.*
>
> *I do not ask on behalf of these alone, but for those also who believe in Me through their word; that they may all be one; even as You, Father, are in Me and I in You, that they also may be in Us, so that the world may believe that You sent Me.*
>
> *The glory which You have given Me I have given to them, that they may be one, just as We are one; I in them and You in Me, that they may be perfected in unity, so that the world may know that You sent Me, and loved them, even as You have loved Me. (John 17:11, 20-23)*

Jesus prayed that we would be one as the triune God is one. Indeed, Jesus prayed that we would "be perfected in unity"—literally, "made complete in unity." And, when His prayer is answered and we become one as Jesus and the Father are one, our *unity through identity* will manifest the fullness of God's glory to the world. Since our Kingdom agenda is to see "the earth filled with the knowledge of the glory of the Lord as the waters cover the sea" (Habakkuk 2:14), unity must be our highest priority.

Paul echoes the eschatological imperative of unity in Ephesians 4. Only as the Church becomes one in Christ can the Body of Christ fully manifest God's glory. Look at the text:

> *Therefore I, the prisoner of the Lord, implore you to walk in a manner worthy of the calling with which you have been called, with all humility and gentleness, with patience, showing tolerance for one another in love, being diligent to preserve the unity of the Spirit in the bond of peace.*
>
> *There is one body and one Spirit, just as also you were called in one hope of your calling; one Lord, one*

> *faith, one baptism, one God and Father of all who is over all and through all and in all. (Ephesians 4:1–6)*

Then, Paul shows how this unity happens:

> *And He gave some as apostles, and some as prophets, and some as evangelists, and some as pastors and teachers, for the equipping of the saints for the work of service, to the building up of the body of Christ; until we all attain to the unity of the faith, and of the knowledge of the Son of God, to a mature man, to the measure of the stature which belongs to the fullness of Christ. (Ephesians 4:11–13)*

Jesus gave apostles, prophets, evangelists, shepherds and teachers to the Church so that we all could be equipped to build up the Body of Christ until "we all attain the unity of the faith." This is why the Church gathers "two or three in His name."

The pursuit of unity also transforms the way we interact with others. As Paul said:

> *Therefore if there is any encouragement in Christ, if there is any consolation of love, if there is any fellowship of the Spirit, if any affection and compassion, make my joy complete by being of the same mind, maintaining the same love, united in spirit, intent on one purpose.*
>
> *Do nothing from selfishness or empty conceit, but with humility of mind regard one another as more important than yourselves; do not merely look out for your own personal interests, but also for the interests of others. (Philippians 2:1–4)*

All of these passages—and many more!—emphasize how central the idea of unity was to the early Church. Their world was even more stratified and divided than ours. First century Christians lived, worked and worshipped every day in a world where Jews and Gentiles would not eat together, women had no rights and thirty to forty percent of the populace was enslaved. No wonder the gospel seemed so revolutionary with its core unity message:

> *For all of you who were baptized into Christ have clothed yourselves with Christ. There is neither Jew nor Greek, there is neither slave nor free man, there is neither male nor female; for you are all one in Christ Jesus. And if you belong to Christ, then you are Abraham's descendants, heirs according to promise. (Galatians 3:27–29)*

Paul understood so well that unity is an eschatological instrument, a mechanism by which the end of history is drawn forward to fulfill the promises made by the prophets. He saw clearly that the unity of Jews and Gentiles in the one Body of Christ would signal the consummation of the ages. In fact, Paul declared that the unity of all things in Christ was what God has been doing since the beginning of time:

> *Making known to us the mystery of his will, according to his purpose, which he set forth in Christ as a plan for the fullness of time, to unite all things in him, things in heaven and things on earth. (Ephesians 1:9–10 ESV)*

Literally, Paul asserts here that the eschatological unity of Jews and Gentiles, slaves and free, men and women, Greek and barbarians into the one Body of Christ would be the catalyst for the perfect union of heaven and earth. Creation will be liberated when the sons of God are manifest. (Romans 8:21) *Heaven comes to earth through the unity of believers!*

Again, God does not bypass people. Reconciled people are the means by which all creation is liberated and united together as one unbroken reality where "God is all in all" (1 Corinthians 15:28). Division is banished in creation as it is banished in you and me.

See why I keep pounding the table on this topic?! Unity is such a big deal that I am not sure we will ever exhaust it.

## *Defining Unity*

What is unity? It's important to answer this question because, in a world shaped by various forms of human supremacy, unity is usually distorted into mere acquiescence around a dominant person. This sort of pseudo-unity is more of a "you do what I say and we'll all get along" kind of unity. And that's not unity at all. That's tyranny.

In Scripture, unity is the unique and significant contribution each person makes to the community as a whole. Unity is you adding your part, me adding my part, until we all discover how to balance our individual contributions. Biblical unity is *unity-in-diversity.*

For power-driven pyramid systems, what they call "unity" is really a squashy uniformity that suppresses individuality into system-approved, personality-squelching little boxes. But in the Kingdom, unity is a result of our mutually-discovered identity in Christ. You discover who you are in Him, and I discover who I am in Him. And we both discover how our personality uniquely manifests the glory of God. My individuality is not measured against you or anyone else. It is measured against how God made *me*. Same for you.

The world's uniformity measures you and me against others. Uniformity becomes conformity. And it's usually the dominant "others" at the top of the pyramid who demand our conformity so they can consolidate and maintain their power over us. Uniformity forces us to become whom others want us to be. Uniformity is rooted in comparison and competition —which fosters insecurity—but not so with Kingdom unity. Kingdom unity is all about people being who they are in relation to God's image in them. Unity flows from royal identity.

Since we are called to manifest the Father individually and uniquely, Kingdom unity only flourishes in an environment of freedom. That's profoundly counterintuitive. Most sociologists would argue that people can only be unified when their freedom is limited by conforming to the group. Think of how the military stamps out individuality in favor of uniformity. Their goal is a "military machine" made of humans. They create a pseudo-unity that works well in an power-driven environment of top-down control. But top-down control is wrong kingdom.

In the Kingdom of God, you and I bring our difference to the table and contribute what only we can give. That sort of unity—that sort of risky freedom—makes religious rulers panic. How can we be sure that everyone does the right thing if we give them freedom? How can we be assured of achieving our unified goals if we do not enforce compliance? And that's where the Kingdom of God comes rip-roaring through the world's control systems like a hurricane.

***Freedom is messy. And unity is messy. Kingdom unity often looks at first glance like chaos. And that gives religious people the heebie-jeebies.***

Freedom is messy. And unity is messy. Kingdom unity often looks at first glance like chaos. And that gives religious people the heebie-jeebies. It takes time for people to learn how to coordinate their freedom and align their efforts around a unified vision. And until they do, it's usually a mess. It is that circle dance we talked about earlier. Everyone has to discover their own steps, their own flow.

The circle dance of Kingdom unity is *perichoresis*. (There's that $5 word again!) As we saw earlier, "perichoresis" is the "interpenetration, interfusion" (literally, "a circle dance") of the internal, eternal life of the Trinity. God the Father, Son and Holy Spirit exist forever within one another. Though there are three "persons" in the Trinity, yet they are one God because their eternal existence co-inheres with each other in mutual indwelling. The Father abides within the Son and the Spirit, the Son within the Father and Spirit, the Spirit within the Father and Son. They do not, indeed *cannot*, exist separately. As theologians like to say, cutting it fine with a precise doctrinal knife, the "persons" of the Trinity are "distinct but not separate."

This, as astonishing as it may seem, is the unity that Jesus invites us to share. This is the unity for which He prayed:

> *That they may all be one; even as You, Father, are in Me and I in You, that they also may be in Us, so that the world may believe that You sent Me. (John 17:21)*

Jesus prays that you and I will be submerged into the unity of the Trinity, that we may be one with Father, Son and Holy Spirit. Most people who pursue serious inner healing know that our wholeness comes from being properly realigned through love with the Father, Son and Spirit. As we become one with Them, we become one with ourself, with our *true self* created in the image of God and hidden in Christ. (Colossians 3:3, 9-14)

And—here's the shocker!—as we become one with God, we become one with each other. (This is how being healed in our relationship to the Trinity heals our relationships with people. Inner healing becomes outer healing.) We not only enter the perichoretic dance with the Trinity, but we enter the perichoretic dance with each other. Jesus not only prayed that we would be one with Father, Son and Spirit, He also prayed that we would be one with each other. Just as we are baptized into Christ, submerged into the internal, eternal life of the Trinity, so we are baptized into one another, submerged into the Body of Christ.

> *For by one Spirit we were all baptized into one body, whether Jews or Greeks, whether slaves or free, and we were all made to drink of one Spirit. (1 Corinthians 12:13)*

When we are baptized into the Body of Christ, we are submerged into the existential life of all Spirit-filled believers everywhere. We become one spiritually with each other.

We must grasp this reality. The Body of Christ is made one by the Holy Spirit poured out from heaven into the hearts of individuals everywhere. The Spirit grasps each individual and submerges them into the shared life of the Trinity. *We are baptized into Christ.* And when we are baptized into Christ, we are baptized into everyone who has been baptized into Him. *Together, we are His Body.* Which means that my baptism into Christ brings me into existential oneness with *you*. Because you are in Christ and I am in Christ, we are in one another. Like fish in the sea, we are all in the water and the water is in all of us. We become one as the Trinity is one.

You and I not only enter the circle dance with the triune God, we enter the circle dance with one another. We share in perichoretic life. Your gifts and callings, talents and abilities are flowing through the Holy Spirit and become available to me through spiritual impartation. (Think of it as spiritual WiFi that connects us on a global network, a heavenly Internet.) Who you are flows into me, and who I am flows into you. Though we remain distinct, we are no longer separate. Your spirit *influences* (flows into) me and my spirit *influences* (flows into) you.

I become more of who I am because your spirit is now accessible to me. You enrich me. And I enrich you. Like instruments in the symphony, our music blends, and we become greater together than we could have been alone. You bring more out of me that God created me to be. In fact, I *cannot* be all I was created to be without you (and others like you), for your individuality enhances my individuality. If you are absent, if you become disconnected, a part of me is unfulfilled. I need you, and you need me.

But this presents a grave dilemma. When I become one with you and you become one with me, we are exposed to each other's pain. And this is where people panic and pull back. Unity is painful. I already have enough pain with my own issues, I don't want to carry yours too. Yet Paul instructs us:

> ***Though we remain distinct, we are no longer separate. Your spirit influences (flows into) me and my spirit influences (flows into) you.***

> *So that there may be no division in the body, but that the members may have the same care for one another. And if one member suffers, all the members suffer with it; if one member is honored, all the members rejoice with it. (1 Corinthians 12:25–26)*

You and I are supposed to share each other's suffering and each other's honor. Which highlights another challenge to unity: we often are willing to share our suffering, but may be reluctant to share our honor. Plenty of blame to go around, but stingy with praise. That seems to be all too common among humans, even Christian humans.

## *Unity Through Honor*

Suffering with each other and rejoicing with each other as Paul envisioned requires holding each other in high regard. I must have a high value for you to be able to walk with you through the ups and downs of life. Otherwise, I walk away. Unity requires honor.

The larger context around the 1 Corinthians 12 "suffering and rejoicing" quote we just read shows how important honor is to attaining and maintaining unity. Look at the entire quote (it's worth your time!):

> *But now God has placed the members, each one of them, in the body, just as He desired. If they were all one member, where would the body be? But now there are many members, but one body.*
>
> *And the eye cannot say to the hand, "I have no need of you"; or again the head to the feet, "I have no need of you." On the contrary, it is much truer that the members of the body which seem to be weaker are necessary; and those members of the body which we deem less honorable, on these we bestow more abundant honor, and our less presentable members become much more presentable, whereas our more presentable members have no need of it.*
>
> *But God has so composed the body, giving more abundant honor to that member which lacked, so that there may be no division in the body, but that the members may have the same care for one another. And if one member suffers, all the members suffer with it; if one member is honored, all the members rejoice with it.*
>
> *Now you are Christ's body, and individually members of it. (1 Corinthians 12:18–27)*

Do you see the centrality of honor here? God gives "more abundant honor to that member which lacked, so that there may be no division in the body" (vs. 24-25). By releasing honor—especially to those for whom honor seems undeserved!—we drive out division. Paul points out that we cover the parts of the body that seem least honorable, the parts that are most embarrassing if exposed. If we step out of the shower and someone walks in unexpectedly, our hands instinctively go to the "private parts" of our body. We show honor by covering nakedness.

Two of the sons of Noah showed honor to their father when his nakedness was exposed, and they received great blessing for doing so. (Genesis 9:20-27) The third son, Ham, was cursed for dishonoring his father by exposing his nakedness. Think about that now: we have been trained by the world to only show honor to the honorable. But Paul teaches us that honor bestowed upon the dishonorable actually confers honor. When we show honor, we release honor. Honor can make the dishonorable honorable.

That's how honor works. And this is how honor increases unity. When I honor you, I refuse to discard you because of your pain. I will walk with you through it. When you sin, I will confront you in love and point you to your true destiny. I will not simply walk away because relationship with you has become difficult. I recognize you as an image-bearing child of the King, and I will hold you to higher expectations. I honor you.

And I need you to do the same for me.

By the way, though our focus here is honor shown to one another, it is also true that we must honor ourselves. Much of the self-abuse and self-destructive behavior marring the human race comes from self-loathing, from a lack of self-respect and self-honor. As we so often point out, Jesus said for us to love our neighbors as ourselves, which assumes, of course, that we must know how to love ourselves. A culture of honor can take root among people who look in the mirror and despise who they see. We must honor the person God made us to be.

Of course, honor requires healthy boundaries. Sometimes people resist the correction honor requires and become toxic. There are times that we must remove ourselves from dangerous relationships, and it is not dishonor to do so. In fact, true honor is perfectly willing to take a firm line with toxic people and refuse to "go along just to get along." Sometimes, we may be forced to withdraw from a person precisely *because* we honor them and refuse to enable their self-destructive and others-destructive behavior.

Paul was clear about this in 1 Corinthians 5 and 6. He addressed the issue of a man in the church who had taken his father's wife to be his own.

> *It is actually reported that there is immorality among you, and immorality of such a kind as does not exist even among the Gentiles, that someone has his father's wife. You have become arrogant and have not mourned instead, so that the one who had done this deed would be removed from your midst.*
>
> *For I, on my part, though absent in body but present in spirit, have already judged him who has so committed this, as though I were present. In the name of our Lord Jesus, when you are assembled, and I with you in spirit, with the power of our Lord Jesus, I have decided to deliver such a one to Satan for the destruction of his flesh, so that his spirit may be saved in the day of the Lord Jesus. (1 Corinthians 5:1–5)*

Paul was flabbergasted. He was shocked that the Corinthians had such a low view of Christ and the Church, of themselves and the man who had sinned, that they would arrogantly celebrate their "freedom" by parading sin up and down the aisles at church. This was not honor—this was presumption.

Paul continued with his loving judgment:

> *I wrote you in my letter not to associate with immoral people; I did not at all mean with the immoral people of this world, or with the covetous and swindlers, or with idolaters, for then you would have to go out of the world.*
>
> *But actually, I wrote to you not to associate with any so-called brother if he is an immoral person, or covetous, or an idolater, or a reviler, or a drunkard, or a swindler—not even to eat with such a one.*
>
> *For what have I to do with judging outsiders? Do you not judge those who are within the church? But those who are outside, God judges.*
>
> *Remove the wicked man from among yourselves. (1 Corinthians 5:9–13)*

**Honor demands accountability.**

Honor demands accountability. Just like a parent holds a beloved child accountable for his or her actions, so we must hold each other accountable. If I am not willing to correct you—and you me!—then I do not truly love you.

Honor is not a hall pass for sin. Not at all. Honor draws the best out of redeemed people. Paul had such a high view of saved people. He declared over the Corinthians:

> *Or do you not know that the unrighteous will not inherit [partake of] the kingdom of God? Do not be deceived; neither fornicators, nor idolaters, nor adulterers, nor effeminate, nor homosexuals, nor thieves, nor the covetous, nor drunkards, nor revilers, nor swindlers, will inherit [partake of] the kingdom of God.*

*Such were some of you; but you were washed, but you were sanctified, but you were justified in the name of the Lord Jesus Christ and in the Spirit of our God. (1 Corinthians 6:9–11)*

Your behavior, Paul says in so many words, should be exemplary because you are exemplary people, though it may seem for now that your exemplariness is more potential than actual. Paul holds them to the high standard of Christ's holiness as he warns them:

*Flee immorality. Every other sin that a man commits is outside the body, but the immoral man sins against his own body. Or do you not know that your body is a temple of the Holy Spirit who is in you, whom you have from God, and that you are not your own? For you have been bought with a price: therefore glorify God in your body. (1 Corinthians 6:18–20)*

Holiness through honor. That's Paul's approach. Because believers are God's temple, because they are "bought with a price," therefore they should "glorify God in [their] body."

Fornication is dishonoring. It cheapens the human body that Christ purchased for His dwelling place. Our body is a holy place. Moreover, fornication disrespects the larger Body of Christ, for—remember?—we are all connected. As Paul put it:

*Do you not know that your bodies are members of Christ? Shall I then take away the members of Christ and make them members of a prostitute? May it never be! (1 Corinthians 6:15)*

Paul does not mean that one believer is personally culpable when another member commits fornication, but he does mean that the Church body is dishonored when one member sins. Remember the Patricia King story? One team member jeopardized the entire mission by consorting with the enemy through lust and addiction. When a member commits fornication, the Body of Christ is infected. (See also 1 Corinthians 3:16-17)

Honor holds people accountable. If we truly see the high value of people, we will expect holiness. But there's a fine line here, for religious people love to "hold people accountable" legalistically under the pretense of love. And that's why the quest for unity through honor can get so messy. There is no exact formula for love. We will often get it wrong. And when we do, we must grab hold of honor with both hands and do the hard work of cleaning up the mess we've made.

Honor refuses a thin veneer of respectability, the pretense of perfection. Like a mother who loves her children no matter what they do, honor embraces people with all their mess and helps them sort it out. When people refuse help, then honor puts up good boundaries and insists on costly love rather than cheap indulgence.

Like the Father of the prodigal son, we do not demand that people stay when they want to leave, but we keep the home fires burning until they come to their senses and wend their way back to the family. And when they do, honor is waiting with a warm hug and a kiss, with a clean robe, a ring of authority and a feast to celebrate that another wayward child has come home.

Honor values people at their best and their worst. Honor deems people worth it. Honor respects individuality and gives people freedom to be themselves. Honor recognizes the value in people, and celebrates them for it. Honor appreciates the image of God manifest in others. Honor sees the God-potential in people and celebrates that the infinite beauty and creativity of Father God is being displayed in them. Honor sees the role we all play in our place.

Kingdom unity flows from honor. When we truly honor one another, our high value for one another prevents us from attempting to control or pigeonhole others. I can align freely with you even if you're quite different than me because I appreciate the image of God in you.

Every one of us has a unique fingerprint and a unique call on his or her life. There is no one else quite like you by divine design. You were created on purpose, to fit perfectly in His Body. Sometimes part of our journey is just to discover what unity-in-diversity looks like. Who are we and how do we fit? And it's a fun journey if we don't let the enemy make us think that we're wrong for wanting to be honored, for desiring that kind of connection, that kind of belonging. It's not wrong to want to join the dance of triune life. We were created for it!

As Paul shows when teaching on the "spiritual" in 1 Corinthians 12, the gifts of the Spirit highlight the infinite variety and complexity of God that is manifest in human individuality. And as Holy Spirit distributes His gifts through our unique personalities, the hardened divisions that fracture the human race are erased: we are no longer separated as "Jews or Greeks, slaves or free" (1 Corinthians 12:13). By allowing people to be themselves and by allowing Holy Spirit to manifest the manifold glory of God in them, we meditate reconciliation to the world.

That's what unity looks like.

## *Submission and Headship*

So then, how does Kingdom unity impact equality between men and women? Simply like this.

God created men and women equal. He created both male and female to manifest aspects of His undivided nature. He never intended for one to dominate the other. The Creator formed male and female in a relationship of mutual submission. It was sin, rooted in a lie, that distorted human relations into a struggle for supremacy.

The male-female relationship started out like this:

> *The man said, "This is now bone of my bones, and flesh of my flesh; she shall be called Woman, because she was taken out of Man." For this reason a man shall leave his father and his mother, and be joined to his wife; and they shall become one flesh. And the man and his wife were both naked and were not ashamed. (Genesis 2:23–25)*

When God created mankind, "the human" (*ha-adam*) was created male and female. The female was hidden inside the *adam*. But God declared that it was not good for the *adam* to be alone. So, He drew the female out of the male and made them distinct. He brought them together and taught them how to be one again spiritually, sexually and covenantally. Now, the part that was missing from the *adam* was rejoined, distinct but not separate.

(We'll talk a lot more about all this in Book 3.)

Then, due to sin, united male-female relationship became this tragic, divided reality:

> *To the woman He said, "I will greatly multiply your pain in childbirth, in pain you will bring forth children; yet your desire will be for your husband, and he will rule over you." (Genesis 3:16)*

What a heartbreaking pronouncement! But thankfully, there's one more scene in the story. Jesus came to restore male and female in the new creation:

> *There is neither Jew nor Greek, there is neither slave nor free man, there is neither male nor female; for you are all one in Christ Jesus. (Galatians 3:28)*

In fact, Jesus came to make things better than before. In Christ, we are not only reunited with each other, we are united to the life of the triune God in a way that was not possible before the incarnation, resurrection and ascension of Christ. By becoming one with us, Jesus made us one with God and changed our origination "from earth" to "from heaven." (1 Corinthians 15:45-50) The new creation is not just a return to Eden—it is literally heaven come to earth, a reality of which Eden was just a signpost.

This means that men and women should be *more* equal, as it were, in the new creation than we were before. More united, more mutually submitted.

Paul grabs hold of this idea in Ephesians 5. Due to our oneness with God in Christ, there is an unprecedented oneness of relation available to male and female, a mutual submission that models, manifests and mediates the "mystery" of Christ's oneness with the Church. Here's Paul's teaching:

***The new creation is not just a return to Eden—it is literally heaven come to earth, a reality of which Eden was just a signpost.***

> *And do not get drunk with wine, for that is dissipation, but be filled with the Spirit, speaking to one another in psalms and hymns and spiritual songs, singing and making melody with your heart to the Lord; always giving thanks for all things in the name of our Lord Jesus Christ to God, even the Father; and be subject to one another in the fear of Christ. (Ephesians 5:18–21)*

The central command, the imperative that anchors the entire text, is "be filled with the Spirit." Every other phrase that follows modifies this command. "Be filled with the Spirit" like this:

- Speaking through singing
- Giving thanks for all things
- Be subject—literally, "submitting"—to one another in the fear of Christ.

Then—and the flow of phrases modifying how we are to "be filled with the Spirit" continues unbroken—Paul drops the command that has been used for so long to suppress women:

> *Wives, be subject to your own husbands, as to the Lord. For the husband is the head of the wife, as Christ also is the head of the church, He Himself being the Savior of the body. But as the church is subject to Christ, so also the wives ought to be to their husbands in everything. (Ephesians 5:22–24)*

The NASB has "be subject" here, but it literally means "be submitted" (*hypotassomenoi*—"mutual, reciprocal submission"). And the first thing to note is that the translators broke the flow of the text. In the original, Paul is still stretching out one of his famous run-on sentences. He is still talking about how we are to be filled with the Spirit. The command to wives here is not a new thought. The command for women to be submitted to their husbands is an extension of the command for everyone to "be submitted to one another" (v. 21). And that must not be overlooked.

Are wives commanded to be submitted to their husbands? Yes, of course. But husbands are also commanded to be submitted to their wives. That is precisely what it means when Paul says, "Be submitted to one another in the fear of Christ." Paul is teaching *everyone* submit to one another in love. Paul then goes on to show what mutual submission looks like for wives and husbands, parents and children, masters and servants.

Paul makes this mutual submission explicit in 1 Corinthians 7 when he talks about the "authority" that a husband and wife have over each other. Which, by the way, is a *radical and revolutionary* idea in the first century. Look at it:

> *The wife does not have authority over her own body, but the husband does; and likewise also the husband does not have authority over his own body, but the wife does. (1 Corinthians 7:4)*

This is what mutual submission looks like. It looks like perichoresis. It looks like mutual honor. It looks like having such high value for each other that we "outdo one another in showing honor" (Romans 12:10 ESV). It looks like "with humility of mind regard one another as more important than yourselves" (Philippians 2:3).

It's time to redeem the concept of submission. Submission is not what religion and culture has made it out to be. Submission was never placed solely on the female gender. Submission was never meant to be enslavement or subjugation. Submission was always meant to be the willing surrender of our heart to one another. The most vivid picture of what submission is supposed to be is the sexual surrender that happens through powerful, mutual love.

Submission is meant to be a safe place where people are free to be who they are truly meant to be. Submission is not about you or me controlling another person. Submission is about you and me giving safe haven for another to let their hair down. When two people are truly submitted to one another, then there is no fear that one will impose his or her will on the other.

Submission is the safety of a child nursing at its mother's breast, the beauty of a bride dancing with her groom, the elegance of an old couple holding hands on a park bench. Submission is a quiet place of total trust. I have nothing to fear because you are submitted to me and I am submitted to you.

So think then of what is lost when submission is twisted into a power play of one person dominating the other. Safety evaporates and freedom vanishes. The man loses his safe place because he must now safeguard his position over the woman. He better watch his back. The woman loses her safe place because now she must fight for every ounce of freedom she can muster. Or worse, she gives up and dies inside like the slave in the first scene of the towel and basin story. When submission is perverted into subjugation, both men and women lose.

Submission has been perverted into a role women must play rather than a relationship she should enjoy. When submission is reduced to a function we must perform, its liberating power is stripped away. When you truly love someone, you have no problem laying your life down for them. You have no trouble placing your life in their hands. You are *submitted* to them.

***Submission is a quiet place of total trust.***

As I mentioned earlier, the translators divided female-submission from everyone-submission in Ephesians 5. Strangely enough, they do it every time. In Ephesians 5, in Colossians 3, in 1 Peter 3. Not only is a new sentence started in each case, but a new verse disrupts the flow. Many translations even add subject headings that make the division between everyone-submission and female-submission complete.

Why? I think the translators are human, and they reflect unconscious bias in their arrangement of the text. I hesitate to impute more insidious motives. Whatever the reason, the impression that women should be subjugated to men is deepened in our hearts as we read Scripture. That's tragic. Father God never intended that to happen. And it's time to change it.

A wife submitting to her husband is a beautiful thing in the right Kingdom context. In the wrong kingdom, it is pathetic bondage. It is like the dehumanized slave we talked about earlier, the one who bent down to wash the master's feet in the wrong kingdom. But in the right Kingdom, submission reenacts the love of Christ as He removed His royal robe and donned the towel to wash His disciples' feet. Submission in this context comes from a place of strength that is eager to serve.

In its proper biblical context, the context established by Jesus' example, submission means to "lay down your life for the good of another." It means to lift another up. Think of a loving son reaching out his hand to escort his frail mother. She leans against him, presses her hand into his arm and walks carefully down the stairs as he upholds her. He is *submitted* to her, but he is not subjugated. He willingly submits his mobility to her out of love. He could rush off down the stairs at a breezy pace and leave her to navigate alone. But he willingly submits. Is he a slave? Only to love. He is free to choose, and he freely chooses to love. This is what submission looks like. Now, if the mother is a domineering matriarch who commands him to escort her against his will, then he loses his ability to choose love and his "submission" becomes slavery.

In the Kingdom of God, submission can only be freely given. That's why Jesus said:

> *For this reason the Father loves Me, because I lay down My life so that I may take it again. No one has taken it away from Me, but I lay it down on My own*

> *initiative. I have authority to lay it down, and I have authority to take it up again. This commandment I received from My Father." (John 10:17–18)*

Do you see the connection between Kingdom authority, freedom and submission? It's all intertwined.

Submission is lifting another up. Which leads us to the next part of Paul's teaching in Ephesians 5: *headship*.

Again, here's how Paul said it:

> *Wives, be subject to your own husbands, as to the Lord. For the husband is the head of the wife, as Christ also is the head of the church, He Himself being the Savior of the body. But as the church is subject to Christ, so also the wives ought to be to their husbands in everything. (Ephesians 5:22–24)*

Just like the idea of submission, headship has been terribly distorted by millennia of misogynistic assumptions. We have imported from the wrong kingdom a definition for headship that does not align with Christ's example. We know that Paul told the men to serve as the "head" of the woman just as Christ serves the Church, but then we conveniently ignore how Christ actually served as the head and redefine headship in terms of wrong kingdom male supremacy.

How is Jesus the head of the Church? As its origin and source. Not as its "boss." (We'll talk more about the meaning of "head" in Book 3 when we spend some time in 1 Corinthians 11.) The hierarchical concept of headship is borrowed from the world's pyramid systems. Jesus showed us what headship looked like when He washed the disciples' feet. Headship looks like you and me giving our lives to lift others up.

Do you remember the painting I mentioned earlier, the one with the male dancer holding his female partner high over his head as she whirled in unbridled ecstasy? That's headship. To be the head of anyone or anything in the Kingdom of God is to come underneath and uphold as loving support. Headship is about enabling others to come into their fullness in Christ. Like the foundation of a house holds up the house, so the head of anyone or anything in the Kingdom upholds.

Submission and headship is a beautiful picture of how Christ lived his whole life. He reigns as head over the Church in perfect submission to His Father's will and in loving submission to us. Jesus knew exactly what submission was like, for He existed from eternity in loving submission to the Father. But never for a moment was God the Son subjugated by the Father. The Church has worked really hard throughout the centuries to prevent that sort of subordinationism from corrupting our view of God. We must work just as hard to eradicate subordinationism from our perichoretic union as the Body of Christ.

> ***One of the most heartbreaking realities we face is that biblical ideas meant to be the steel framework for unity have been twisted into crowbars that pry us apart.***

Mutual honor is mutual submission. Perichoresis is experienced only though mutuality. Mutual submission flows from honor. How can men and women be united in Christ if men display contempt toward women by subjugating them?

Misogyny is dishonor.

Misogyny is divisive.

Misogyny is demonic.

Submission and headship were intended to be liberating concepts, beautiful pictures of what it means to imitate Christ by laying our lives down for one another. One of the most heartbreaking realities we face is that biblical ideas meant to be the steel framework for unity have been twisted into crowbars that pry us apart. Submission and headship were meant to unite us, but through satan's instigation, once again, what should unite us divides us. It's time to cast that devil out!

# CHAPTER 11

# THE TEMPLE

One of the most powerful metaphors of unity through identity is the temple of God. Several of the themes we've discussed so far converge in the temple: love, service, cooperation with God, a "non-pyramid" structure, royal identity, nobility, dominion, submission and headship all resonate through the walls and halls of the temple. But unity is the idea that constantly comes into the forefront when studying the temple. The temple is the intersection of heaven and earth, the place where God and all nations come into perfect union.

## *The Recurring Temple Motif*

The temple of God is made of people. When Jesus came, He brought into new covenant reality what the old covenant had foreshadowed. The physical temple in Jerusalem with all its sacrifices and services had always been a symbol of a greater reality to come. God desired to dwell within people. As He said:

> *"Heaven is My throne and the earth is My footstool. Where then is a house you could build for Me? And where is a place that I may rest? For My hand made all these things, thus all these things came into being," declares the Lord. "But to this one I will look, to him who is humble and contrite of spirit, and who trembles at My word." (Isaiah 66:1–2)*

God's dwelling place is the humble worshipper. So when we read about the temple of God in the New Testament, we must hold in mind the perichoretic union of God with His people.

Paul, as usual, is the one who draws the most vivid comparisons between the temple and Spirit-indwelled people. Paul uses three primary metaphors for the congregation of Christ's followers: the Bride, the Body and the Building. He uses all three together in Ephesians, mixed up like a Greek salad. Paul opens with the body metaphor in Ephesians 1:22-23, which leads into the "one new man" in 2:15. But just before the "one new man" statement, Paul starts warming up his temple imagery:

> *For He Himself is our peace, who made both groups into one and broke down the barrier of the dividing wall. (Ephesians 2:14)*

Christ is the peace treaty between the warring factions, the Jews and Gentiles, who were famously hostile to each other. But Christ has made "both groups into one" and joined them into His global temple. Though Paul does not explicitly mention the temple here, the "barrier of the dividing wall" makes it clear that he is thinking in temple terms. The "dividing wall" with its blatant warning sign barring Gentiles stood within the temple courts at Jerusalem, which Paul had seen countless times, and it prohibited Gentiles from entering fully into the presence of God. Now, in Christ, Paul declares, both Jews and Gentiles are invited all the way in.

Paul does a quick u-turn back to the body metaphor for a few verses (vs. 15-17), and then comes roaring back to one of the most powerful temple passages in the New Testament:

> *So then you are no longer strangers and aliens, but you are fellow citizens with the saints, and are of God's household, having been built on the foundation of the*

*apostles and prophets, Christ Jesus Himself being the corner stone, in whom the whole building, being fitted together, is growing into a holy temple in the Lord, in whom you also are being built together into a dwelling of God in the Spirit. (Ephesians 2:19–22)*

The Gentiles are "no longer strangers and aliens," but they are now welcome to join with the congregation of faithful Israel as they worship the one true God manifest in Christ. Gentiles have become "fellows citizens" and are now "God's household," the Father's House, as Jesus once described the temple. This new temple, made up of both Jews and Gentiles, is built upon the "foundation of the apostles and prophets" with Jesus as its cornerstone.

Then, Paul unleashes a barrage of "unity phrases":

- In whom the *whole building* (the "whole" being Jews and Gentiles together)
- Being *fitted together* is growing into a holy temple in the Lord
- In whom you also are being *built together* into a dwelling of God in the Spirit

The *whole building* is *fitted together* and *built together.* The emphasis on unity is unmistakable. And no wonder! Paul was tasked with cobbling together profoundly disparate groups into one coherent, Spirit-filled congregation. No easy task. And the building of the temple, with Paul no doubt leaning on his recollection of how Solomon's temple was constructed, provided a great framework for Paul to cast the vision of a united Church.

As Paul saw it, Jews and Gentiles were like stones placed together, perfectly aligned with Jesus, the corner stone, and with each other. Peter echoes the same idea:

*You also, as living stones, are being built up as a spiritual house for a holy priesthood, to offer up spiritual sacrifices acceptable to God through Jesus Christ. (1 Peter 2:5)*

Both Peter and Paul see believers as the stones that make up the temple, the priests who offer sacrifices and the sacrifice itself. The swirl of temple-worship metaphors is almost dizzying.

Paul also uses the temple-worship metaphor in Romans 12:

> *Therefore I urge you, brethren, by the mercies of God, to present your bodies a living and holy sacrifice, acceptable to God, which is your spiritual service of worship. (Romans 12:1)*

***And believers, joined together in unity, are the priests who "present" their bodies as a sacrifice. This unified priestly presentation is our "spiritual service of worship."***

Here again, believers are the sacrifice and the priests. The temple is not mentioned explicitly, but it is implied. Where else are sacrifices offered? But what's really interesting here is that Paul envisions the sacrifice as one combined sacrifice made up of many believers: "present your *bodies* (plural) a living and holy *sacrifice* (singular)." Paul's use of plurals and singulars is just one more example pointing to the unity of Christ's body—Jews and Gentiles are many bodies, but one sacrifice. And believers, joined together in unity, are the priests who "present" their bodies as a sacrifice. This unified priestly presentation is our "spiritual service of worship."

Paul repeats the idea with similar phrasing in Romans 15 when he describes himself as a "minister of Christ Jesus to the Gentiles, ministering as a priest the gospel of God, so that my offering of the Gentiles may become acceptable, sanctified by the Holy Spirit" (Romans 15:16).

All of Paul's *Epistle to the Romans* is written to promote unity between Jews and Gentiles.

- In Chapters 1-8, Paul lays out the theology of unity: we are justified by grace through faith, not by circumcision and law-keeping, and thus no uncircumcised Gentile believer should be excluded.
- In Chapters 9-11, Paul deals with the exclusivity of Israel as God's covenant people and what Gentile inclusion meant for the faithfulness of God to Israel. Had God failed Israel? Or forsaken Israel? Not at all.
- Then, Chapters 12-15 are Paul's attempt to weave all his arguments together as a rationale for why Jews and Gentiles should be able to gather together at the Lord's Table and share union and communion as one.

Right after opening Romans 12 with the call to sacrificial and priestly unity, Paul wades off into how the Church operates as one:

> *For through the grace given to me I say to everyone among you not to think more highly of himself than he ought to think; but to think so as to have sound judgment, as God has allotted to each a measure of faith.*
>
> *For just as we have many members in one body and all the members do not have the same function, so we, who are many, are one body in Christ, and individually members one of another.*
>
> *Since we have gifts that differ according to the grace given to us, each of us is to exercise them accordingly: if prophecy, according to the proportion of his faith; if service, in his serving; or he who teaches, in his teaching; or he who exhorts, in his exhortation; he who gives, with*

*liberality; he who leads, with diligence; he who shows mercy, with cheerfulness. (Romans 12:3–8)*

Then, verse after verse, through four more chapters, Paul addresses how the Church should worship and do life together as one. Though it's often overlooked, the entire letter to the Romans was all about unity. That's the heart of everything Paul wrote in this, his magnum opus.

One point that we should mention here is that Paul's vision of unity in Romans was not just between Jews and Gentiles. Paul also saw the united temple as a powerful model for unity between men and women. Though Paul does not mention gender equality specifically, his passion for it expressed elsewhere hums underneath every phrase in Romans.

This becomes evident in Romans 12 and then explicit in Romans 16. In Chapter 12, Paul runs through a list of unity behaviors, as quoted above:

*Since we have gifts that differ according to the grace given to us, each of us is to exercise them accordingly: if prophecy, according to the proportion of his faith; if service, in his serving; or he who teaches, in his teaching; or he who exhorts, in his exhortation; he who gives, with liberality; he who leads, with diligence; he who shows mercy, with cheerfulness. (Romans 12:6–8)*

The message of unity between men and women here is somewhat obscured because the translators, working from their implicit bias again, use masculine pronouns: *his* faith, *his* serving, *his* teaching, *his* exhortation, *he* who gives, *he* who leads, *he* who shows mercy. But the original Greek here is gender inclusive. It should be rendered "us" and "they" throughout. Though the translators' bias tragically hides Paul's intent, this passage is actually a powerful statement of gender unity within God's holy temple. Men and women together are the living stones that edify the global temple.

The idea of gender unity continues in Paul's thought throughout Chapters 12-15. But when we get to Chapter 16, Paul's implicit assumption of gender equality becomes an explicit celebration of women in leadership. Starting with Phoebe the deacon to Junia the apostle and numerous women in between, Paul celebrates women in Romans 16 in the most overtly pro-female passage in the New Testament.

Do you see my point? The one living sacrifice of Romans 12:1 is made up of both men and women. The priesthood that offers the sacrifice is both men and women. And the temple in which the sacrifice is offered is made up of both men and women. The temple is a powerful metaphor for male-female unity. So if the women of God are segregated and silenced, then the dividing wall of hostility is erected once more and Christ is divided. As Paul would say, God forbid! May it never be.

## *The Tabernacle and the Temple*

As I mentioned, Paul most likely wrote about the temple with Solomon's Temple in mind and, undoubtedly, the Tabernacle of Moses. Paul also would have definitely had the temple at Jerusalem, the one he had visited countless times, in the back of his mind. Indeed, there is no way to exaggerate how important the temple-history was to devout Jews. To Jews, the temple was the site of God's physical presence on the earth. They believed that the temple was the actual intersection of heaven and earth, the place where the veil between the visible and invisible grew paper-thin.

In fact, devout Jews saw the temple as the cosmos in miniature. They believed that the universe was God's macrocosmic temple, and the temple on earth was a microcosm of heaven. When they peered from a safe distance into the dimly lighted interior of the Holy Place as the priests ministered, they believed they were getting a glimpse into what heaven was like. They believed that the earthly temple was a model of heaven. (Hebrews 8:5)

As *The Epistle to the Hebrews* shows throughout, the Jews who came to faith in Jesus, the first Christians, came to understand that Jesus was the ultimate reality to which the temple pointed. Jesus *was* the temple of God, the tabernacle of His presence. And when Jesus baptizes believers with the Holy Spirit and the Holy Spirit baptizes believers into the Body of Christ, they become the corporate extension of Him. Which means that believers become the temple of God both individually and corporately.

> ***Christians are microcosmic manifestations of God's temple in the world. We are little "heavens" walking around on earth. And heaven breaks through us into the world.***

So, for first century believers, Christians are microcosmic manifestations of God's temple in the world. We are little "heavens" walking around on earth. And heaven breaks through us into the world. That means that the reality foreshadowed by the temple is now actualized in us.

This is how Paul saw the temple. Everything that the temple portrayed pointed to Christ and us in Him. Paul and his fellow Christians studied the temple closely so that the shadowy types of Christ would become clear through the illumination of the Holy Spirit.

Take a close look at Hebrews. It shows that the first Christians studied the structure and liturgy of the temple to understand more about Christ. They studied the gates and doorways. They studied the courts of the Lord, the walls and curtains. They pored over biblical descriptions of the outer court, the inner court and all the furnishings of the temple. They meditated on the meaning of the brazen altar and the brazen laver, which both stood in the outer court. They wrestled through the hidden meanings of all the various sacrifices and offerings. They now saw all of that in light of Christ and His death for our sins.

They entered slowly through their imaginations into the Holy Place, the first section of the inner sanctum. They wandered carefully around in their minds, picturing the seven-branched Golden Candlestick with its carefully tended supply of oil; the Table of the Presence, where the bread and wine were refreshed daily; and then, right in the center, just before the huge veil that separated the Holy Place from the innermost chamber of the Holy of Holies, stood the Altar of Incense, symbolizing the prayers and praise of the saints.

No doubt, early believers would then pause mentally just outside the veil and reach through with their mind's eye to where the Ark of the Covenant nestled securely under the Mercy Seat, overshadowed by the wings of the vast cherubim of pure, beaten gold. There in the Ark would be the pot of manna, Aaron's rod that budded and the Ten Commandments.

For first century Christians this imagined scene would have looked quite different than it did in reality for Old Testament priests because when Christ died, a holy angel (or perhaps Yahweh Himself) ripped the veil from top to bottom and the way into the Holy of Holies was opened for one and for all. No doubt, Christians would have lifted their hands in worship, tears flowing freely, as they mentally pictured the reality the torn veil conveyed. The way into the heavenly temple was now open to all.

I think I can relate in a teeny-tiny way to how they would have felt. I had a vision of the temple—well, it wasn't a movie sort of vision, but more like a series of pictures scrolling by. It was sometime in 2005, and I was with a group of friends at a women's conference in Florida. In between one of the sessions, my friends were out in the lobby at one of the book tables, and I stayed in my chair just lingering and worshipping a bit.

Suddenly, this series of pictures burst into my mind, one after another. I followed them across the screen of my mind, and then asked as I often do, "Okay, Lord, is that you?" The pictures were of me standing in the outer court of the temple. Then, from the edge of my vision, the scene changed and the Lord led me from the outer court into the inner court of the temple. I glanced beside me, and was slightly startled to see the Lord standing beside me dressed formally like a groom, top hat and all. I then realized that I was dressed as a bride. Strange.

Then I thought, "You know, this is kind of cool!" I looked around at the furniture of the outer court. It all seemed so familiar after years of studying it. In fact, I felt pretty confident at this point. Sort of like, "I got this!" I was about to get quite a surprise.

The Lord took my hand and walked with me past the various elements of the tabernacle, the altar and laver, and as He did, I started thinking about how He was my sacrifice—the One now holding my hand!—and how He was now calling me to lay down my life as a living sacrifice. Quite sobering, but so deeply joyful.

Then He took me into the Holy Place. Actually, He picked me up like a groom would a bride and carried me over the threshold of the Holy Place. When the flap of the tent closed behind me, the scene before me completely took my breath away. It was like I was carried directly into a revelation of His love. It was a very romantic setting. In fact, if you think about the Holy Place, it is a beautiful candlelight dinner. The seven-branched candlestick, burning with oil, illuminates the bread and wine on the Table of His Presence, and the sweet aroma of incense radiates slowly from the Altar of Incense in the middle of the room, standing back against the heavy curtain.

The Lord carried me over to the table, and immediately I knew that it was the table of communion and connection with Him, where we receive His body and His blood and become one with Him. He carried me over by the candle stand, and I knew so deep that the Word was illuminated by the Holy Spirit—burning, burning, burning!—and I knew it would burn hot in me.

Then He took me to the Altar of Incense standing at the back of the room against the great veil that concealed the Holy of Holies. I stiffened in His arms and tried to draw back just a bit. I suddenly felt a keen sense of inadequacy. "Time out!" I protested. "I don't know how to properly approach the Lord in worship. Help me, O Lord! I don't understand worship." Then an astonishing thing happened. The Lord quickly sat me back down on my feet. He looked at me with a long, penetrating gaze, and then He grasped the Altar of Incense and pushed it firmly—almost fiercely!—through the heavy veil.

All I could think of in that breathtaking moment was, "Holy moly!" (Which, I suppose at least, my moly was holy!) I was almost paralyzed with reverence. Then—swish!—the veil was gone. Utterly gone. Now, there I was in the Holy of Holies without having to walk through the veil. All because the Lord pushed the Altar of Incense, which represents prayer and worship, through the veil. The incense from the altar was rising, merging with the glory cloud of His presence. It was utterly breathtaking!

And in one profound instant, I knew what He meant to show me: prayer and worship carried me through the veil, but it was not something I achieved in my own strength. He did it. And that was the point: I didn't do it—He did it! He showed me in that moment that worship cannot be worked up. Prayer is not performed through our strength and effort. Worship and prayer are done as *He* does it for us and in us. The breakthrough happens when *He* fiercely shoves the altar through. He does the work in us!

Then the scene faded, and I was left with a profound sense of His presence. What an experience! It was totally transformative. It revealed how intimate, even romantic, the presence of God is. He showed me that prayer and worship are less about religious striving and more about an easy, intimate relationship. He demonstrated to me so vividly that prayer and worship are not about my performance, about me being an expert in temple protocols. It is about being carried by the Lover of my soul. It is about allowing Him to bring my prayers and worship before the throne.

Several months later, I was reading in Hebrews 9, and I suddenly realized that the Altar of Incense is described in the wrong place. In the Old Testament, the Altar of Incense stood outside the veil in the Holy Place where daily ministry was done. But the writer of Hebrews clearly states that it was placed inside the veil within the Most Holy Place.

I was puzzled over this for a bit, and then it hit me: that's exactly what Jesus did at Calvary! He pushed the Altar of Incense through the veil, He opened up the way for all to enter in. He did it for us! His Spirit carries us through into

His presence and into oneness with Him without fleshly striving and struggling to achieve it on our own. Jesus opened the way to oneness with the Father by grace through faith. Not a striving faith as many of us fall into, but rather a resting faith. Jesus will do the heavy lifting. Union with God is a gift that we freely receive.

And the key to that easy entrance is Spirit-born and Spirit-borne worship. Worship is not work that we do out of strenuous performance. Worship is rest. Worship is yielding. Worship is simple submission to His love. Worship is surrender.

And that's why I say that I can relate to the early Christians who passionately explored the mysteries hidden in the temple. Only eternity will unveil them all!

***And worship is the one thing that can transform the hearts of men and women and eradicate forever the false supremacy that divides us.***

## *Worship and the Temple*

The temple is built for worship. And worship is the one thing that can transform the hearts of men and women and eradicate forever the false supremacy that divides us. We've talked a lot about the heart because that's the only way the Kingdom is unleashed—through the regenerated heart.

Worship transforms the heart. As we behold the beauty of the Lord, we are transformed into His image. As Paul put it:

> *But whenever a person turns to the Lord, the veil is taken away. Now the Lord is the Spirit, and where the Spirit of the Lord is, there is liberty.*

> *But we all, with unveiled face, beholding as in a mirror the glory of the Lord, are being transformed into the same image from glory to glory, just as from the Lord, the Spirit. (2 Corinthians 3:16–18)*

As we worship—as we behold the glory of the Lord—we are transformed into the image of God in Christ. Worship manifests identity. Worship reveals who God is to us and who we are in Him. Worship grounds us in the glory of God. Worship strips away the pseudo-identity formed through the fear of man and unleashes who we really are in Him.

Isaiah experienced a powerful revelation of identity, both God's and his, as he worshipped in the temple. (Isaiah 6:1-8) He saw the Lord "sitting on a throne, lofty and exalted." Isaiah caught a vision of God as King of all creation. And the throne on which the Lord was seated was the Mercy Seat within the Most Holy Place. Isaiah watched as the angels flew back and forth crying, "Holy, Holy, Holy, is the Lord of hosts, the whole earth is full of His glory." Then the foundations of the house trembled at the presence of God.

As Isaiah collapsed in fear and dread at the holiness of the Lord, he cried out, "Woe is me, for I am ruined! Because I am a man of unclean lips, and I live among a people of unclean lips; for my eyes have seen the King, the Lord of hosts." Worship just became real. Isaiah saw himself without the artificial accretions of identity gathered through a lifetime of people-pleasing. His false self-image shattered, and he saw himself naked and afraid.

But the shattering of Isaiah's false image simply made way for a revelation of his true identity before God. God was about to show Isaiah how *He* saw him. An angel flew by the altar and grabbed a coal from the altar with a pair of tongs. He touched the burning coal to Isaiah's lips and declared, "Behold, this has touched your lips; and your iniquity is taken away and your sin is forgiven." Then, after being liberated from false identity, Isaiah was commissioned as a prophet to the nations.

What a powerful story! But the main point I want you to see is that worship was the catalyst for heart change. And the same is true today. When we gather in the temple as the temple, as the priests and as the sacrifice, we are joined together as one Body, one Bride, one Building. And as we worship, centuries of generational mindsets drop away in the glory of His presence. Our hearts are transformed, and we are formed into one community of faith.

In Book 1, I talked about how Holy Spirit said to me, "The hearts of men are now ready." I think a huge part of preparing the hearts of men for the *unity through identity* movement that is now happening has been the global release of worship over the last few years. As we worship in the temple, we begin to worship *as* the temple, the unified habitation of God through the Spirit. As we worship the one true God, we are made one. As Paul argued in Romans 3, the oneness of the people of God is derived from God's own oneness.

> *Or is God the God of Jews only? Is he not the God of Gentiles also? Yes, of Gentiles also, since God is one—who will justify the circumcised by faith and the uncircumcised through faith. (Romans 3:29–30 ESV)*

Here's Paul logic: since the God of both Jews and Gentiles is one, then the Jews and Gentiles must be one. The oneness of God unites them. That takes us right back to John 17 and Jesus' prayer: "That they may be one, just as We are one" (John 17:22).

And this is how worship unifies us as the temple of God. We submit our hearts to the one true God. And as our hearts are all submitted to Him, our hearts come into alignment with each other. Our submission to Him becomes submission to one another. That's the mutual submission we talked about earlier.

We are united in the temple as priests ministering together. We are united in the temple as one sacrifice offered on the altar. And we are united in the temple as the temple itself, the living stones that experience mutual submission through the interlocking, interdependence of perichoretic construction. Every stone depends on the other to remain strong and stable.

Worship is a powerful expression of submission. In fact, worship means "to bow down" and "to dwell on someone's *worth-ship*." Worship brings an understanding of worth, of value, of honor. To worship is "to give homage." See how the temple ties together all we've discussed?

***Our submission to Him becomes submission to one another.***

The first time the word "worship" is used in Scripture is in Genesis 22, which is the story of God commanding Abraham to offer his beloved son, Isaac, as a sacrifice. Abraham arrived at the foot of Mt. Moriah where the sacrifice was to happen and:

> *Abraham said to his young men, "Stay here with the donkey, and I and the lad will go over there; and we will worship and return to you." (Genesis 22:5)*

"We will worship." Abraham described his submission to the most difficult divine demand he had ever faced as "worship." What an incredible expression of faith!

As you know, Isaac was not put to death that day. God was never interested in human sacrifice. The Lord wanted to share with His friend a secret He'd been dying to tell for years: salvation will come through the substitute offering of Christ, the beloved Son of God.

But the main thing I want to emphasize here is that worship is submission. Worship is holding nothing back. Not even the thing that we hold most dear. Worship is hearing God and obeying. Worship also means to fear God, to reverence and trust Him.

Worship is submission, and it produces mutual submission among those who worship together. But worship never compels submission. Submission that is demanded does not originate in worship. Worship flows out of freedom. Forced worship is not really worship at all. As I said before, forced submission is rape. And that's not love.

God does not demand worship. He draws us to worship through love. He woos us into worship, but He does not demand worship. In fact, as He showed me in the vision where He sat me down and He moved the altar for me into the Holy of Holies, worship is a movement of the Spirit within us, not effort we work up out of our own strength.

Worship is rest.

Worship is yielding.

Worship is surrender.

And as we worship like this, the urge for supremacy melts away. I really believe deep in my heart that true worship will continue to grow in the earth, transforming the hearts of men (and women) in every nation under heaven so that male supremacy will melt away like snow in bright spring sunshine. When we gather together as the temple of God, His presence makes us one. Women are liberated and the Kingdom is unleashed. Worship makes it happen.

## *Cleansing the Temple*

Now, why does all this matter? Simply because the unity of Christ's Church is the only way that the Kingdom can come throughout the nations. As Paul said:

> *Now may the God who gives perseverance and encouragement grant you to be of the same mind with one another according to Christ Jesus, so that with one accord you may with one voice glorify the God and Father of our Lord Jesus Christ.*
>
> *Therefore, accept one another, just as Christ also accepted us to the glory of God. For I say that Christ has become a servant to the circumcision on behalf of the truth of God to confirm the promises given to the fathers, and for the Gentiles to glorify God for His mercy; as it is written, "Therefore I will give praise to You among the Gentiles, and I will sing to Your name." (Romans 15:5–9)*

When we have "the same mind" and "with one accord...glorify God"—when we "accept one another" as "Christ also accepted us"—then the Gentiles will "glorify God for His mercy." Just as we saw earlier, the unity of the Church attracts the world to Christ.

In Paul's day, the division was primarily between Jews and Gentiles. These days, our unity issues are more along the lines of race and gender. (Though the Jewish-Gentile divide persists and will be fully reconciled when "the fullness of the Gentiles has come in" [Romans 11:25].) Our focus here is gender, of course, but wherever the fault-lines lie, we must see every breach healed and unity come to the Body of Christ.

Think about this now: the temple is the place where we should be most united. But the sad truth remains that the temple of God, the congregation of believers throughout the nations, is exactly where believers are most divided. As Malcolm X used to say regarding race relations and the Church, there is no hour more segregated in America than Sunday at high noon. The same is true about gender.

As I said in Book 1, I experienced equality as a young woman for the most part at work and in the world around me. But when I came into the Church, I found that the glass ceiling is mostly stained glass. We have seen women find equality in education, in the workplace, in politics, in media and culture. So much progress has been made. But the Church still sanctifies male supremacy and calls it "biblical complementarianism." And that means that the worship of the one true God is hindered by our unwillingness to break the shackles of misogynistic culture.

> ***It is time for women to fully share in the royal priesthood that has been dominated by men.***

It's time for Jesus to cleanse His temple. And He will do so through us. He will cleanse the temple through us as we turn over the tables of tradition and cast out the merchants of misogyny. (And I mean, cast out their ideas, of course. I'm not advocating the excommunication of complementarians. Just to be clear.) The temple of the Most High God cannot be complete as long as half the living stones—the female ones!—are left out of place and disconnected. It is time for women of God to be set in place.

It is time for the dividing walls of hostility to be broken down, for they *are* broken down in Christ. No more will the temple of God accommodate the old, outdated "Court of the Women" that sequesters women outside full inclusion in the temple of God. No more.

It is time for women to fully share in the royal priesthood that has been dominated by men. And I don't mean only vocational ministry as "professional clergy," though that's included in what I mean. No, the royal priesthood is the priesthood of *all* believers, an idea that Protestant Christianity has professed to believe but failed to live out. By excluding women from leadership, we have been limited from fully unleashing the Kingdom in the family, the Church, in business and everywhere else humans gather to do life.

The royal priesthood is made up of believers, both men and women, who have been called as kings and priests with Christ. The idea of "royal priesthood" blends the essential responsibilities of dominion and worship given to all Christians. In fact, we cannot see dominion come fully in the earth apart from restored, Spirit-filled, gender-equal worship. The worship of the one true God is what mediates the oneness of God into the world.

The royal priesthood gathers for worship as the habitation of God through the Spirit. That gathering is called "the ekklesia," which is the Kingdom assembly of King Jesus. The ekklesia is His parliament. But the parliament of King Jesus is also His temple. The temple of the King is also His throne room. His temple is His palace. Worship and dominion merge in the temple of God.

The Kingdom of God cannot be unleashed as long as the worship of God's people is segregated for any reason. As long as we divide by race and gender, by class and political persuasions, the temple of the Most High God is fractured. And since the temple is God's palace, His government cannot be extended in the earth apart from royal worship. The royal priesthood must be fully integrated in every way. The Body of Christ must be united as one.

God will inhabit the earth through His temple, His holy people formed into perfect unity with Him and one another. And that perfect unity remains imperfect as long as women are shut out of leading and serving as royal priests in the Father's House. As living stones, men and women are aligned to Him and to one another. In fact, there is no better picture of the mutual submission we discussed above than the interlocking stones of the temple. The strength of the temple and the stability of the stones comes from from their union with each other. Each stone finds its fulfillment in its alignment to the others. In the temple, we find *unity through identity.*

# CHAPTER 12

# THE GREAT MYSTERY

The subjugation of women has often been established on Scripture texts that point to wives being subject to their husbands as the Church is to Christ. The most famous (or infamous!) passage is in Ephesians 5:

> *Wives, be subject to your own husbands, as to the Lord. For the husband is the head of the wife, as Christ also is the head of the church, He Himself being the Savior of the body. But as the church is subject to Christ, so also the wives ought to be to their husbands in everything. (Ephesians 5:22–24)*

We spent some time redefining and redeeming submission and headship in Chapter 10, but I think we need to come back here for one more swing at it. There's another layer to Paul's teaching that needs deeper explanation.

First of all, as we noted, "be subject" means "to submit" mutually and willingly into the loving care of another. Submission in the Kingdom is never forced. And submission is never meant to serve the supremacy of any person over another. Moreover, submission is commanded for everyone—Kingdom submission is *mutual submission*.

Headship is all about supporting and upholding others. The word "head" here means "source, or origin." Remember the male dancer upholding the female?

But all of this comes into clearer focus when we actually look at how Jesus serves as head of the Church and how the Church actually lives out submission. The misogynistic, male supremacist culture that has developed around us looks nothing like Christ and the Church.

If the Church is the Bride of Christ, then does Christ forbid His Bride to speak? Does He forbid her to lead? Does He demand that she sit by in silence while He does all the speaking, teaching, leading? Does Christ subjugate His Bride? Does He reduce her to powerlessness and refuse her the right to own property, have a say in decisions, or speak to Him while passing Him in the street? Does Jesus treat His Bride with dismissive contempt like the Chaldee spirit we talked about in Book 1?

I think not. Jesus loves His Bride, died to save His Bride, and then empowered His Bride with the Holy Spirit so that she could actualize full dominion over creation. That doesn't sound much like an only-males-lead "complementarian" relationship!

Jesus' goal for His Bride is that she should share in His glory. He desires that His Bride should be seated with Him on His Father's throne. Jesus' longing for the Church is that the Church should be one with Him and the Father. Jesus has no desire to keep His Bride shoved meekly into a corner. Jesus wants His Bride to be crowned with Him, to rule and reign with Him forever. Jesus longs for His Bride to have dominion, to conquer and subdue all creation until the entire universe blossoms fully with the glory of the Lord.

That's the sort of headship Jesus provides. That's the sort of submission He expects. And that sort of headship and submission looks nothing like the kind of headship and submission imposed on women for millennia. So how about we stop pointing to Christ and the Church as the model for misogyny? It doesn't work anymore.

## *Marriage and Mystery*

Just a few verses after declaring that wives must submit, Paul pulls the pin on one of the most explosive statements in Scripture:

> *Christ also [loves] the church, because we are members of His body. For this reason a man shall leave his father and mother and shall be joined to his wife, and the two shall become one flesh. This mystery is great; but I am speaking with reference to Christ and the church. (Ephesians 5:29–32)*

> ***Reconciled marriage actually releases the love of Christ for the Church into the world. Healed male-female relationships become the catalyst for healing across the spectrum of human relationships.***

Just when we thought Paul was only handing out practical advice to improve the quality of family life, he lobs an unexpected revelation: "This mystery is great; but I am speaking with reference to Christ and the church." Of course, Paul was giving practical advice for the family, but underlying it all was a much deeper meaning. The male-female relationship that lies at the heart of marriage is intended to model, manifest and mediate into the world the love that Christ has for the Church.

Paul does not mean to say that marriage only resembles the relationship between Christ and the Church as mere imitation. No, he means to say that reconciled marriage actually releases the love of Christ for the Church into the world. That's what I mean when I keep saying that healed male-female relationships become the catalyst for healing across the spectrum of human relationships. If we can get this one right, every other relationship will have a model to follow.

A Kingdom marriage mediates grace. When a marriage comes into alignment with the supernal love of Christ for the Church, that alignment becomes a channel through which grace flows. When a husband learns how to love his wife as Christ loves the Church; when a wife learns how to live in free, mutual submission as the Church does with Christ; when a husband learns how to submit to his wife; and when the wife learns how to love her husband; then, and only then, can the power of the misogynistic curse be exposed as a lie and expelled forever.

This is the great mystery. The oneness of Christ and the Church takes root in the culture through the oneness of Christian marriage. When the Church is transformed into oneness, then the family is transformed. And when the family is transformed, culture is transformed.

We've been going at it backwards. We've tried to reform culture by focusing on political, social, educational, technological and economic action. And all those things are important. But until the foundation stones of culture are repaired—the Church and the family—we are simply pasting wallpaper over crumbling walls. And it also doesn't do us any good to reform politics, business and family while leaving the Church as the last bastion of male supremacy due to a deep misunderstanding of Scripture.

This is why I keep crying out for a cleansing of the temple! The relationship between Christ and the Church mysteriously mediates oneness. And if we allow the enemy to maintain a stronghold in the Church, then the source—the Head, if you will!—of oneness is blocked.

The theme of mystery is all throughout Ephesians. Paul first mentions "the mystery" in Ephesians 1:

> *He made known to us the mystery of His will, according to His kind intention which He purposed in Him with a view to an administration suitable to the fullness of the times, that is, the summing up of all things in Christ, things in the heavens and things on the earth. (Ephesians 1:9–10)*

The "mystery of His will" is "the summing up of all things in Christ." Or, as the ESV puts it, "a plan for the fullness of time, to unite all things in him, things in heaven and things on earth" (Ephesians 1:10 ESV). Do you see that? The mystery is all about uniting all things in Christ. The perichoretic oneness of all things in Christ has been God's mysterious plan from the start.

Paul mentions the mystery again in Ephesians 3. He calls it "the mystery of Christ" (v. 4). He then explains that "this mystery" (v. 6 ESV) is "that the Gentiles are fellow heirs and fellow members of the body, and fellow partakers of the promise in Christ Jesus through the gospel" (Ephesians 3:6).

Then Paul calls the rule of King Jesus:

> *The administration of the mystery which for ages has been hidden in God who created all things; so that the manifold wisdom of God might now be made known through the church to the rulers and the authorities in the heavenly places. (Ephesians 3:9–10)*

King Jesus governs the "administration of the mystery." And His strategy is to reveal the mystery "through the Church" so that all the "rulers and authorities in the heavenly places" may behold "the manifold wisdom of God." Literally, Jesus is unleashing His Kingdom authority over the spirit-systems of the world through the oneness manifest in the Church.

What is the mystery? That God has made all things one in Jesus. Jews and Gentiles, slaves and free, male and female, black and white, rich and poor—on and on. And that mystery, that all things are reconciled in Christ, is revealed in the mystery of marriage. The unity of Christ and the Church flows out to the family. As men and women reproduce the union of Christ and the Church, the harvest of reconciliation bears fruit in the world.

Do you see why the revelation of the mystery is such a big deal?

The mystery is that all things are one in Christ. All things find their identity in perichoretic union with the triune God. The first hint of this mystery was hidden in Adam and Eve. In the Garden, male and female were one. Something of the female was already inside the *adam* (*ha-adam*), but male and female were undifferentiated and thus the human was alone. God declared that this was "not good." So God surgically distinguished the male and female so they could be joined again as distinct but not separate, just like the Trinity.

***The mystery is that all things are one in Christ. All things find their identity in perichoretic union with the triune God.***

God drew the female out of the human and fashioned her into what Adam called the "woman" (*ishshah),* which means "out of man" ("man" is "*ish*"). Adam prophetically declared:

> *This is now bone of my bones, and flesh of my flesh; she shall be called woman, because she was taken out of man. For this reason a man shall leave his father and his mother, and be joined to his wife; and they shall become one flesh. (Genesis 2:23–24)*

From the first moment, the *adam* manifested the mystery. Their unity-in-diversity was a living picture of what reality was like. Everything created proceeds out of the Creator by His Word and then returns to be one with Him in a divine circle of perichoretic union. Yet God does not absorb the individuality of His creation into Himself. Differentiation and individuation permit assimilation without annihilation.

Whew. That was a mouthful.

This unity-in-diversity is what the world is like because it is what God is like. The mystery of the Trinity, how God can be three-in-one, lies at the heart of all mystery. The "mystery of godliness" (1 Timothy 3:16), as Paul puts it, is the mystery manifest in Christ and the Church—we are one in Him!

## *The Power of Covenant*

The creational reality of unity-in-diversity is held together by the covenantal love that unites Father, Son and Holy Spirit. Because God is love, there is no chance of division within Him. The Trinity exists in perfect covenant with each other, which is what holds all things together. Love fills the space between. The covenant is binding.

And that unity is what the covenant of marriage is meant to actualize. When a man leaves his father and mother, he "cleaves," as the KJV puts it, to his wife. This "leaving and cleaving" is covenantal language. The man is differentiated from his family of origin and assimilated into his new covenant reality. He becomes *one flesh* with her.

The man and woman become one flesh in covenant union (literally, a *corporation*), one flesh in sexual union and one flesh in their children. They become three-in-one—husband/wife/child. This is a vivid picture of the triune God and the triune reality of all things created by Him. (Space/time/matter, to point out just one example of triune reality.)

This, by the way, is why a marriage covenant is so important. The covenant forms a lasting framework for unity-in-diversity as a husband and wife pledge to keep faith with another. And it is within the safety of that fidelity pledge that perichoretic love can flourish.

Marriage is a blood covenant. In the Garden, when God put Adam to sleep, He brought the woman out of his side. When God split Adam's side open to draw out the woman, the first blood was shed. (Does that remind you of anything? It reminds me of the blood and water gushing out of Jesus' side on the cross as His Bride was brought forth.) And even today, when a couple become one flesh in sexual union for the first time, blood and water are shed as her hymen is broken. It will be broken one time and one time only. It is a blood covenant.

The mystery of marriage is the mystery of union, of how two people become one. And that's why male supremacy is such a violation of the mysterious union of male and female. Just like rape is a horrific violation of the blood covenant, so male supremacy is a violent disruption of the triune nature of God manifest in marriage.

Malachi roared against this sort of violent male-domination in Malachi 2. The prophet started off with—wouldn't you know it?!—the oneness of God:

> *Do we not all have one father? Has not one God created us? Why do we deal treacherously each against his brother so as to profane the covenant of our fathers? (Malachi 2:10–17)*

Then, Malachi launched into a fiery tirade against chauvinist men:

> *This is another thing you do: you cover the altar of the Lord with tears, with weeping and with groaning,*

*because He no longer regards the offering or accepts it with favor from your hand.*

*Yet you say, "For what reason?" Because the Lord has been a witness between you and the wife of your youth, against whom you have dealt treacherously, though she is your companion and your wife by covenant. But not one has done so who has a remnant of the Spirit. And what did that one do while he was seeking a godly offspring?*

*Take heed then to your spirit, and let no one deal treacherously against the wife of your youth. "For I hate divorce," says the Lord, the God of Israel, "and him who covers his garment with wrong," says the Lord of hosts. "So take heed to your spirit, that you do not deal treacherously." (Malachi 2:13-16)*

God refused to hear the men's prayers because they violently suppressed their women. (Peter must have had this warning in mind in 1 Peter 3:7.) They were treating the wife of their youth, the wife of their covenant, "treacherously." The word there for "treacherously" literally means "to cover." ("To cover up, to be covert, to be deceitful, to be unfaithful, to offend.") The chauvinist men were veiling the women's glory. They obscured and concealed their glory. They treated the women with contempt and dishonor. They did not permit the women to manifest the image and glory of God.

"Has not one God created us?" Just like Paul points to the oneness of God to validate the unity of Jews and Gentiles in Christ, so Malachi points to the oneness of God to validate equal treatment for women. Even God's statement, "I hate divorce!" is a denunciation of inhuman treatment of the women by violent men. It's not that God always opposes divorce—sometimes divorce is a righteous response to sin. (Infidelity, for example. See Matthew 19:9.) But God always hates the mistreatment of women, and the divorces happening in Malachi 2 were unjust and abusive toward women who had no way to support themselves other than remarriage or prostitution.

When men overshadow women like that, when they handle them "treacherously," they are covering up the God-imaging identity women were created to reveal. Male supremacy is not just treachery toward women—it is treachery toward God. The violence that covers female glory through subjugation is also covering the divine glory. It is God's image that is hidden, His glory that is concealed, His power that is diminished.

## *Unveiling the Glory*

Often in our wedding traditions, the groom lifts the bride's veil at the conclusion of the vows and reveals her beautiful face to the waiting crowd of friends and family. Everyone gasps when they see her dazzling smile and the flushed joy on the groom's face as he leans in to kiss his bride.

***The violence that covers female glory through subjugation is also covering the divine glory. It is God's image that is hidden, His glory that is concealed, His power that is diminished.***

This ancient tradition is meant to echo the unveiling of Eve's glory when the Creator presented her to Adam. From the beginning, the glory of the man was meant to be shared with the woman and the glory of the woman shared with the man. Mutual submission was meant to release mutual glory.

The removal of the veil is also meant to signify the ending of the couple's former identity with their family of origin and the formation of a new, covenantal union as one. The tearing of a veil or garment in Scripture often signifies the removal of one government and the establishment of a new one. That's exactly what happens in a wedding when the man "leaves his father and mother and cleaves to his wife," to use the KJV phrasing again. The removal of the veil signifies a new governmental union has been formed.

The removal of the veil also hints at the later removal of clothing that allows full intimacy, just as the kiss is a discrete public sign of private sexual union to come. The oneness formed in covenant "before God and all these witnesses" is consummated later in physical oneness. The unveiling of the bride and groom in their marriage chamber should signify the beginning of a mutual vulnerability in nakedness that can only be described as mutual submission.

The passionate beauty of *The Song of Solomon* captures this idea so well. Song of Solomon 4 in particular describes how the glory of a bride is unveiled by her lover. And all of it is meant to convey the love Jesus has for His Bride and His Bride for Him. The mysterious love of Christ for the Church, depicted so poetically in song, is meant to convey how God feels about His people and how He views male and female relationships within the covenant of marriage. The last thing God would have tolerated in Solomon's Song would have been the treachery Malachi decried so vehemently.

The writer of Proverbs describes the sexual union of a man and woman as a mystery "too wonderful for me."

> *There are three things which are too wonderful for me, four which I do not understand: The way of an eagle in the sky, the way of a serpent on a rock, the way of a ship in the middle of the sea, and the way of a man with a maid. (Proverbs 30:18–19)*

This mystery is the mystery of oneness.

The mystery of Christ and His Bride is revealed (*apokalupsis*) in the *Book of Revelation*. John was invited to behold the glory of Christ's Bride unveiled in Revelation 21-22. Here's what he wrote:

> *Then I saw a new heaven and a new earth; for the first heaven and the first earth passed away, and there is no longer any sea. And I saw the holy city, new Jerusalem, coming down out of heaven from God, made ready as a bride adorned for her husband.*
>
> *And I heard a loud voice from the throne, saying, "Behold, the tabernacle of God is among men, and He will dwell among them, and they shall be His people, and God Himself will be among them, and He will wipe away every tear from their eyes; and there will no longer be any death; there will no longer be any mourning, or crying, or pain; the first things have passed away."*
>
> *Then one of the seven angels who had the seven bowls full of the seven last plagues came and spoke with me, saying, "Come here, I will show you the bride, the wife of the Lamb." And he carried me away in the Spirit to a great and high mountain, and showed me the holy city, Jerusalem, coming down out of heaven from God, having the glory of God. Her brilliance was like a very costly stone, as a stone of crystal-clear jasper. (Revelation 21:1–4; 9-11)*

How beautiful!

By the way, did you notice that the heavenly city, the New Jerusalem, is the Bride of Christ? Another example of jumbled up metaphors—the Bride and the Building are one. We could stay there for a while working through that powerful revelation.

But the main thing I want you to see is that the book called *The Revelation of Jesus Christ* (Revelation 1:1) rises to a crescendo in its grand finale with a revelation of His Bride. Do you see that? It is the glory of Christ to glorify His Bride.

And that's what Jesus is doing now. He is restoring glory to His Bride and to women everywhere. Women are worth it. The Body, the Bride and the Building are all ways of showing the unity through identity that belongs to all of us in Christ, women included. Jesus is unveiling the glory of His Bride by unveiling the glory of women everywhere. Jesus is cleansing His temple and rooting out male supremacy. The hearts of men are now ready!

Everything that the triune God is, Christ and the Church are. And everything that Christ and the Church are, husbands and wives are called to be. The mystery of the union within the Godhead is released through Christ and the Church into husbands and wives, and from them into children everywhere —who then carry that union out into the world. Once again, I am not exaggerating one smidgen when I shout to the top of my lungs: reconciliation between men and women will unleash reconciliation into the world.

It really is true.

# CHAPTER 13

# HER CORONATION

After five years of wandering through a Kingdom wilderness—which was a beautiful, wonderful journey!—Holy Spirit started bringing me back to a more direct focus on women's issues. Not that I ever stopped learning about women's issues, for that's what the Kingdom journey was all about, but during those five years I learned how the Kingdom of God is unleashed through unity of men and women. And I learned that the gospel of the Kingdom cannot be secondary to the equality message. The gospel of the Kingdom is the *heart* of the equality message. The only way to change the world is to change the heart.

As Holy Spirit was bringing my half-decade Kingdom excursus to a close—"Ladies and gentlemen, please prepare for landing!"—I had a powerful encounter with Father God that brought even more clarity and urgency to my mandate to proclaim the Kingdom message of unity in Christ.

In April 2010, I attended a conference where Kris and Kathy Vallotton were guest speakers. In a staff meeting, Kris and Kathy both prophesied over me. In a powerful moment of direction and affirmation, Kris said,

> Susan, the Lord is taking a staff out of your hand and He's putting a sword in it. This is David's transition —from leading sheep to fighting Goliath. The Lord is giving you a sword. There's a righteous anger that keeps coming up in you, and you don't know what's wrong. But there's nothing wrong.

When Jesus overturned the tables, He said, "Zeal for Your house is consuming Me." And there's a thing for social justice that is rising up in you that is so strong, it's scaring you. You're actually wondering, "Is there something wrong with me?" These bouts of rage are coming from the Lord. With this whole thing of social justice, your role is shifting, and you're moving from a shepherd to a warrior.

(That's interesting, because most of the team are moving from being warriors to being shepherds. It's [like] what I was talking about with Bill saying, "I don't want to teach anymore." But I feel like it's my greatest season of teaching.)

You're taking on this different role; you're becoming a warrior. The shepherd is becoming a warrior. It's in your right hand. Psalm 98:1 says, "In his right hand, His holy arm brings the victory." The left hand holds the merciful, loving arm of the Lord. That would be more natural for you. But the right hand holds the justice and warring arm of God. And that's what's happening with you. You're turning into a warrior.

You should study the life of Joan of Arc. If you study the life of Joan of Arc—and she didn't live very long, nineteen years, but the length of her life doesn't matter—you'll understand the next five years of your life.

Kathy's word over me was short and to the point, but so powerful: "I keep seeing royalty over you, as well as authority in the area of governmental structure." With all I had been learning about the Kingdom, Kathy's word was like an electric jolt. I knew that Father God was training me in the Kingdom for more than just correct theology, and this was confirmation: He was training and authorizing me for a specific Kingdom assignment.

Of course, Kris's word about Joan of Arc stuck in my head. Then, to make Joan of Arc stand out to me even more, I received another, confirming word about Joan of Arc not long after Kris gave me the assignment to research her. I was at a "Prophetic Explosion Day" one Sunday, and in the middle of a powerful word, a lady I had never met said this:

> I'm hearing "Joan of Arc." And I don't really know her story, but I keep hearing that phrase. I see you as a Joan of Arc, geared up and armored up. Your armor is not heavy steel armor that most warriors wear. It's very comfortable—you even sleep well in it. And I just see this Joan of Arc on a horse, raising her banner and going forth into the things that He has called you to go into.
>
> And I was getting that scripture that says "Though the horses are prepared for battle, it is the Lord who gives the victory" (Proverbs 21:31). You're prepared; you're on a strong, trained horse. But just know that it doesn't matter how prepared or unprepared you sense that you are, the Lord has His victory for you.

That got my attention! The Joan of Arc motif was definitely highlighted in my heart. So I did my homework and learned all I could about Joan of Arc.

## *Joan of Arc*

What I found was fascinating. Joan of Arc was a young woman who lived in fifteenth century France during the Hundred Years' War and led the French to an astonishing victory over the English. She was later martyred by the English in the name of pure religion, which was actually nothing more than a hypocritical coverup for raw political corruption.

Joan, often called *The Maid of Orleans*, was just a teenage girl when she led the French to victory. Indeed, she was only twelve years old when she first started dreaming of her role in restoring France's rightful king. It all began when she started hearing heavenly voices while praying out in the fields. Joan's mother had trained her to be deeply religious, and as she prayed she started receiving direct revelations of the future.

Joan's father disapproved of her "pretensions," as he saw her visions, and forbade her traveling to Chinon to see Charles VII, the rightful king of France. Finally, Joan persuaded her uncle to take her to a nearby town where she then persuaded Robert de Baudricourt to give her an escort to Chinon to see the king.

Joan's journey took her escort and her through hostile Burgundian territory, French communities aligned with the English, so at the suggestion of local people sympathetic to her cause, Joan dressed as a male soldier. This began a habit of dressing as a man that would later become the grounds for criminal charges against her, the crime of "cross-dressing," a violation of Deuteronomy 22:5.

Joan's persistence carried her through, and she met with Charles VII. He was profoundly impressed with her due to prophetic words that she spoke over him privately from visions she had seen. The words she spoke to him in private have never been repeated, but it was enough that Charles threw his support fully behind her.

Joan led an army to Orleans, where, after a long wait, she won a decisive victory. Joan was a hero to the French and a devil to the English. The English believed that she was demon-possessed, and when Joan was later captured in battle by French Anglo-sympathizers, she was handed over to the English to be tried in a farcical, rigged ecclesiastical trial. Joan was convicted of cross-dressing and eventually burned at the stake at only nineteen years old. Joan's case was reopened by Pope Callixtus III, and she was fully exonerated and later declared a saint by the Roman Catholic Church.

Joan remains a powerful symbol to women everywhere. In one sense, she is to the women's movement what Rosa Parks is to the civil rights movement, a young, ordinary woman who turned the world upside with a simple, unexpected act of courage. Both Joan and Rosa stood against the dominant systems of the world, and though both paid a high price for their courage, yet their simple acts of defiance pushed back centuries of oppression and opened doors for women and minorities everywhere.

It is no coincidence that Joan of Arc was canonized by the Catholic Church in 1920, the same year that American women obtained suffrage, securing the right to vote in American politics. It seems to me that Joan's story set something in motion that we are still living out today.

I had to pause after reading all that. This girl, the Maid of Orleans, heroine of the Hundred Years' War, martyr to male-dominated religious power, is the woman that Holy Spirit on two different occasions wanted me to consider as a Kingdom role model. That's astonishing. And humbling. And exhilarating! Joan of Arc was a nobody who changed the world. Maybe I—and you!—could do the same.

I believe deeply that world transformation will come through ordinary people. Ordinary people who discover they are *not* ordinary at all. People like Joan of Arc who hear the voice of God and willingly, even stubbornly, follow. People who are willing to abandon false humility, the humility that affords itself the luxury of fraudulent modesty, a humility that pretends to be too small to make a difference.

I know what I'm talking about. I remember when Holy Spirit started telling me that I had a great call on my life, that I was *special*. For some reason, I had been conditioned to believe that confidence in the call on my life was actually pride, that true humility would never push its way forward into a passionate ambition for the Kingdom. I had been trained to believe that aspirations for greatness in the Kingdom were proud ambitions. But Holy Spirit was determined to call me into a higher purpose, into my royal identity.

He is doing the same for you.

***World transformation will come through ordinary people. Ordinary people who discover they are not ordinary at all.***

Once, when wrestling with royal identity, I had a vision. In the vision, Holy Spirit clearly told me that I was *special* to Him. When He said that, I recoiled. I was not happy at all about being called special. Indignation rose up in me, followed quickly by shame and anger. I thought somehow that if I was special, then others were not. To be special, I had to be better than others. See, my concept of *special* was rooted in comparison with others. I thought Holy Spirit was somehow insinuating that I was superior to others, and I knew that was pride. So I drew back in shock and dismay.

Then, Holy Spirit gently whispered, almost chuckling it seemed, "Susan, don't you know that I am big enough and good enough to love everyone as if they are the only one?" And you know, at that moment, I got it. My *special-ness* comes from His love for me, not from my superiority to others. I am not measured in comparison to anyone. I am only measured by His love for me. Which means that *you are special too!*

We all share in royal identity. Our specialness comes from Him. We are all a Joan of Arc in our own assigned area of influence. We all have a battle to fight, a victory to win, and we are all called to hear His voice and expel the enemy. We are called, like Joan, to crown the rightful king. That is our mandate as the Church. To rally the army. To unite the nation. To drive out the enemy and exalt King Jesus on His rightful throne, right? That's our calling.

And I mean this message specifically for women, even young girls, who feel marginalized and overlooked. You may feel like a young peasant girl wandering alone and afraid across the fields of insignificance. But you are a Joan of Arc. You are a warrior princess, a King-crowner, a regime-overthrower, an enemy-expeller. You are a world-changer.

You are called to royal identity. It's not anything you can earn, you already have it. You are special because God is your Father. Period. You hear a voice in your head, but it's the right kind of voice, the voice of God Himself. You have visions, and those visions are snapshots of the future. You have a driving passion to see the Kingdom come, to see the King enthroned. You are guided by prophetic words that call out your true identity. You are filled with the power of the Holy Spirit. You are called, you are chosen, you are faithful.

You are Joan.

And it's time to rise up.

## *The Story of Esther*

Long before Joan of Arc, there was in the Bible a young Joan-like figure in her own right, the beautiful Queen Esther. Esther was a Jewish girl chosen to be queen in the place of

Vashti, the Persian queen who refused to accede to her husband's demand to show off her beauty before his nobles. The king was incensed and deposed Vashti to prevent the women of Persia from uprising against their husbands after the defiant queen's example.

The men of Persia were desperate to protect their power over women. They were terrified that Vashti's rebellion would lead an insurrection. Tyrants always tremble when the oppressed arise. But they were so afraid that they banished Vashti forever and chose a new queen in her place.

By divine providence, Esther was chosen to be the new queen. She was called by God to be queen in Vashti's place so that the people of Israel could be saved when Haman, the enemy of all Jews, conspired to enact the first worldwide pogrom, the first global Jewish genocide. Because God placed Esther in the kingdom "for such a time as this," as her uncle, Mordecai, put it, the Jews were saved worldwide. What an incredible story!

But there's something else I want you to see here.

Several years ago when I read this story again, I was struck by something I had not seen before: the king's palace was in Susa, the heart of Chaldean culture. I stopped for a moment and blinked. I remembered the dream I had about my dog, Priscilla, and the sheet on the clipboard that said she had "C-H-A-L-D-E-E." (I told all about the dream in Book 1.) And I'll be darned if the story of Esther isn't set deep within the heartland of Chaldee.

Catching my breath, I read back through Esther 1, slowing down to absorb the now obvious misogynistic statements.

Here's how the cowardly men whined (Esther 1:17–22):

- For the queen's conduct will become known to all the women causing them to look with contempt on their husbands.
- This day the ladies of Persia and Media who have heard of the queen's conduct will speak in the same way to all the king's princes, and there will be plenty of contempt and anger.
- When the king's edict which he will make is heard throughout all his kingdom, great as it is, then all women will give honor to their husbands, great and small.
- Every man should be the master in his own house.

Esther was not only there to save the Jews. She was placed within the heart of Chaldean culture to be a Joan of Arc against misogyny. She stands as a sign to women everywhere that we can infiltrate the halls of power and bring the love of Christ to bear against the Hamans of hate and prejudice. We can advance the Kingdom through love so completely that the highest realms of power are influenced by feminine faithfulness.

And where are our Mordecais, the men who recognize that the time has come, that godly women are a new generation of Esthers, called to bring hope and healing into the most exclusive domains of power? It is time for Kingdom men and women to join forces and stand against the Hamans of the world, the Chaldeans who seek to annihilate a righteous generation from the earth.

Woman of God, you have been called to the Kingdom for such a time as this! Like Roger Bannister, the athlete who broke the four minute mile when everyone said it could not be done, we can break the glass ceiling everyone says cannot be broken—especially the one with stained glass.

In fact, I believe the truth of the gospel calls us to recognize that *there is no glass ceiling*, that it is imaginary, a lie told by the serpent to enslave us again. The glass ceiling was shattered in the death, burial and resurrection of Christ. When He ascended up on high, He broke through every barrier to dominion and enthroned us with Him in heavenly places. If there really was a glass ceiling, it would be under our feet. Sort of like Cinderella's glass slippers!

The enemy doesn't want you to learn the truth about the glass ceiling. He wants you to always think that limits are hanging over your head so that you will never learn that the liar belongs under your feet. If the enemy can keep you focused on what you don't have, he will make you overlook what you do have—*dominion!*

Satan remembers quite well the promise that the seed of the woman would crush his head and that there would be enmity between the woman and him forever. No wonder he hates women! Satan is the ultimate misogynist. This is why he works so hard to keep women oppressed under the heel of male supremacy—for as long as women are under man's heel, satan is not. What better way to avoid being crushed than to shove females under the boot of domination?

It's time for us to see what's at stake.

The Kingdom of God was never meant to be a theory. Or mere theology. The Kingdom was intended to be lived out in the real world. The Kingdom was meant to be incarnational, Word made flesh. The Kingdom was meant to be the presence of the King manifest through us. The Kingdom was meant to be supremely practical, life-changing and world-transforming.

The Kingdom was never meant to be sequestered in church buildings. The Kingdom is meant to take root in the world through the loving influence of transformed people.

The Kingdom is a seed that takes root in a changed heart and bears fruit in a changed world. We should be able to see the Kingdom coming in the world. When the Kingdom is fully manifest it is measurable, visible, tangible.

I am not interested in simply winning an argument about equality or just getting more women in pulpits. I am interested in changing the world. I am interested in unleashing the kingdom. That's what my Kingdom journey was all about.

# CHAPTER 14

## HOW THE KINGDOM LIBERATES WOMEN

The Kingdom of God liberates women by radically restructuring power in the world. That's the Big Idea that I'm driving home in Book 2. As I noted above, we cannot skip past this understanding. As Holy Spirit said to me, as I meandered slowly on my five-year journey through Kingdom theology, male and female relations cannot be properly understood and properly restructured until we realize how wrong our fundamental concepts of power really are.

We can reorganize career paths, restructure families and clear the way for women to rise to the top, but as long as "the top" is the goal—as long as we define success as reaching the top of the pyramid—we are simply pressing women into the same corrupting power structures that enthroned male supremacy for so long. And female supremacy is no better than male supremacy. It's not like women make better tyrants. Ending tyranny altogether is our Kingdom aim.

What have we learned about the Kingdom so far?

First, we learned that the Kingdom is here now. We are not waiting for some far-off, future forever to see the restoration of the original creation order God established when He placed humans in the garden as co-regents with Him. The rule of God that began in the garden is the same rule that Jesus came to restore. When Jesus came preaching "the gospel of the Kingdom," it was the Good News that the rule of God was being announced throughout every nation as *here right now*.

We learned that the Kingdom of God comes into the world through *love* and not *power*. We saw this modeled and mediated through Jesus' humble service to His disciples when He washed their feet. The King served His servants!

We learned that love always offers choices. Freedom lies at the heart of God's Kingdom rule. The Sovereign God has chosen to delegate dominion over the earth to humans, and God completely trusts the power of His love to influence free human decisions and guarantee His eternal purpose. As Paul said, "In love He predestined us to adoption as sons through Jesus Christ to Himself, according to the kind intention of His will" (Ephesians 1:4–5). God's will flows from His love.

We learned that the Kingdom of God is not a pyramid structure that gathers all power to those at "the top." Jesus is the corner stone of God's everlasting Temple, not its cap stone. He deliberately placed Himself at the foundation, at the bottom, of the Kingdom structure and aligns every believer in relation to Him and to one another through love.

We learned about royal identity and nobility, that we are already named and claimed in Christ. We learned that we are no longer paupers, but kings. And as we discover who we are, it changes how we live in the world. We live and love from a place of royal identity.

We learned about taking dominion and standing together as one. We learned about the temple of God and how we serve in it as kingly priests. We learned about the great mystery of how all things are already one in Christ and that unity through identity is God's great agenda. It's all He's doing in the world!

Then, we wrapped up with Joan of Arc and Esther, two women who inspire us to act with dauntless courage, women who call us to follow the Groom's voice wherever He leads. We boldly proclaimed that we are called to the Kingdom for such a time as this. We will not quail, we will not falter, we will not accept defeat—for defeat was already defeated at the cross!

(To throw in an old, terrible joke: the serpent was already de-feet-ed. Sorry.)

If we believe all that—and we do!—then can you imagine how male and female relations will inevitably change? No more will we justify power structures that place men over women. We are in a Kingdom where "under" and "over" are intentionally flung aside. We will never again justify male supremacy, for supremacy itself has been nailed to the Cross.

I ask you: in a Kingdom where the King washes the servants feet, how can we defend households where women are reduced to servants and men rule with impunity? In a Kingdom where love offers choices, how can we imprison women for a lifetime—no, for a *thousand* lifetimes!—in systems that offer *zero* choices? How can we worship a triune God who exists eternally in a perichoresis of love and then force our wives and daughters into a form of indentured servitude?

***We will never again justify male supremacy, for supremacy itself has been nailed to the Cross.***

And then what about the Church? How can we defend the oppression of women in a worldly, Chaldee system of silence when Paul so clearly celebrated that, in the Kingdom:

> *There is neither Jew nor Greek, there is neither slave nor free man, there is neither male nor female; for you are all one in Christ Jesus. (Galatians 3:28)*

Paul doesn't mean, of course, that male and female gender distinctions no longer exist, but that the hierarchical systems of the world that fragment humanity have been broken down in Christ and a new, cosmic unity has been released from heaven to earth. We are one! This is the sort of oneness, the kind of unity, into which we all—men *and* women—were baptized. And this is the unity of the Spirit that Jesus died to guarantee.

The bottom line is this: the Church cannot change the world as long as the world keeps changing the Church. As long as we keep adapting our leadership structures to fit the pyramid models of the world—as long as we keep allowing that toxic, Chaldee spirit to infect us—the Kingdom of God cannot bring healing to the nations.

I am not exaggerating just to make a point. I truly believe with all my heart that the Kingdom, with its Temple-model, corner-stone-not-cap-stone leadership, its perichoresis of divine love, is meant to transform every leadership structure in the world. Families, churches, businesses, corporations, governments, organizations of all types, must be reshaped by the Kingdom of God until the power-hungry, pyramid schemes of the world are banished forever.

It is no coincidence that the emancipation of enslaved people led to the emancipation of women, which is now leading to a total restructuring of power in the world. The sad shame, though, is that the Church has to be dragged kicking and screaming into the Twenty-first Century. All because we have interpreted Scripture according to an old, poisonous Chaldee mindset.

It's time for the Kingdom to come! It's time for the clash of kingdoms to break through the anti-Christ power structures of the world. It's time for the Kingdom of God to influence the mountains of culture. It's time for the Church to lead the way into freedom. Freedom for all—men *and* women.

**EQUIPPING PEOPLE TO UNLEASH THE KINGDOM.**

Gregory & Susan Dewbrew founded *Kingdom Brewing* to develop resources for equipping people to unleash the Kingdom of God in every realm of life—family, church, business and culture—until we see a new Kingdom renaissance. If you are passionate about seeing the Kingdom take root in every nation, then join the renaissance. It's the adventure of a lifetime! Learn more at **kingdombrewing.com**.

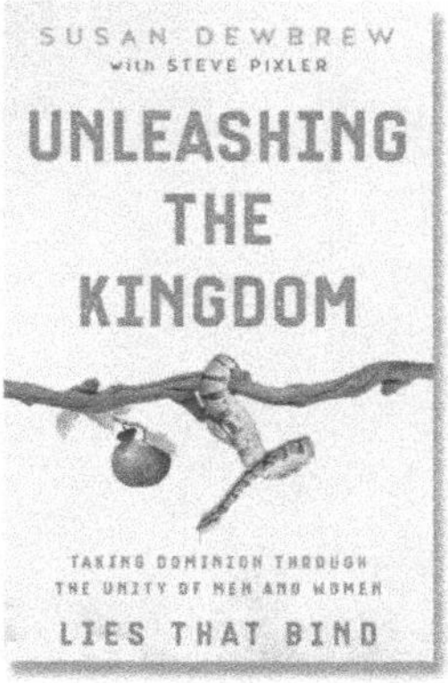


**READ ALL THREE BOOKS IN THE SERIES!**

AVAILABLE AT KINGDOMBREWING.COM OR AT YOUR FAVORITE BOOKSELLERS.

## MORE RESOURCES FROM KINGDOM BREWING

Want to go deeper? Sign up today for **UNLEASHING THE KINGDOM ONLINE COURSE** at kingdombrewing.com.

Want daily encouragement? Sign up for the **DAILY VITAMIN** with Gregory Dewbrew at kingdombrewing.com.

Steve & Jeana Pixler live happily ever after in Mansfield, TX with their six lively children. Steve & Jeana, with an amazing team of Kingdom influencers, lead Freedom Life Church in Mansfield, TX.

To learn more about Steve & Jeana and to discover more Kingdom resources available from their ministry, visit **stevepixler.com**.

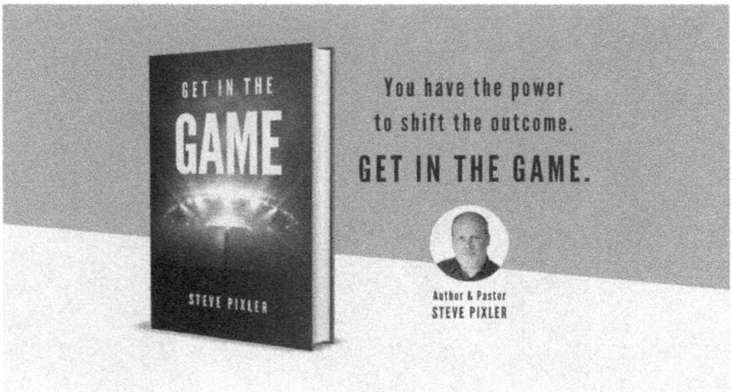

## NOTES

# NOTES

# NOTES

CPSIA information can be obtained
at www.ICGtesting.com
Printed in the USA
BVHW070208090821
613969BV00005B/34

9 781737 221616